Taste*of*Home

5INGREDIENT COMFORT FOOD

TASTE OF HOME BOOKS • RDA ENTHUSIAST BRANDS, LLC • MILWAUKEE, WI

Taste of Home

TRADE ISBN: 978-1-62145-737-4
DTC ISBN: 978-1-62145-741-1

EXECUTIVE EDITOR: Mark Hagen
SENIOR ART DIRECTOR:
Raeann Thompson
SENIOR EDITOR: Christine Rukavena
ART DIRECTOR: Maggie Conners
DESIGNER: Jazmin Delgado
DEPUTY EDITOR, COPY DESK: Dulcie Shoener
COPY EDITOR: Cathy Jakicic

COVER
PHOTOGRAPHER: Mark Derse
SET STYLIST: Melissa Franco
FOOD STYLIST: Josh Rink

PICTURED ON COVER:
Skillet Mac & Cheese, p. 84

PICTURED ON TITLE PAGE:
Maple-Bacon White Chocolate Fudge, p. 206

Printed in USA
1 3 5 7 9 10 8 6 4 2

CONTENTS

P. 109

P. 225

P. 47

SHORT ON TIME?

Keep an eye out for these handy icons to help you quickly identify recipes that fit your schedule.

Fast Fix Dishes are table-ready in 30 minutes (or less!)—from the time you open the fridge to when you put the meal on the table!

Freeze Make-ahead dishes include instructions for freezing and reheating.

MORE WAYS TO CONNECT WITH US:

P. 52

P. 210

P. 123

HOW DO YOU COUNT TO 5?

You'll notice throughout this book that some recipe lists run longer than five lines. That's because there are a few items we don't include in our five-ingredient counts. These are essentials that are so basic we feel comfortable assuming every kitchen always has them on hand. What are they? There are five items on the list, some of which you can customize as you wish.

1. WATER

2. SALT

When we say "salt," we're referring to traditional table salt, and we don't count it. Many cooks regularly use kosher salt instead, preferring it for its more predictable "pinch" measure—feel free to do so. But if a particular recipe requires kosher salt, we'll name it specifically and include it in our count.

3. PEPPER

Black pepper is a go-to kitchen staple, and we don't count it. However, if a recipe demands freshly cracked black pepper, we will name it and count it. Cracked pepper gives the freshest flavor, but not everyone owns a pepper mill.

4. OIL

Three oils make our "don't count" list: vegetable oil, canola oil and regular olive oil. Vegetable and canola oils are highly versatile and can be used interchangeably. They don't have a strong flavor and do have a high smoke point, which makes them ideal for frying, sauteing and baking. Regular olive oil adds a hint of fruity flavor and can be used for light sauteing and roasting, and for dressings and sauces. Extra virgin olive oil, on the other hand, has more specialized uses due to its low smoke point and will be specified (and counted!) when it's needed for a recipe.

5. OPTIONAL INGREDIENTS

We also don't include optional items when counting ingredients. We view these items as suggestions—either as garnishes or as complements—but they aren't necessary to make the recipe, so you can easily leave them out. And, you can always swap them for your own preferred finishing touches.

5 TIPS FOR MAKING THE MOST OF 5 INGREDIENTS

1. THINK FRESH. Many of the most famous classic dishes have short ingredient lists and rely on a few distinctive flavors to carry the day. Start with quality ingredients and don't overcook, and you won't need a lot of extras.

2. CONSIDER COMMERCIALLY AVAILABLE INGREDIENTS THAT PILE ON THE FLAVOR. Jarred sauces, packaged rice mixes, seasoning blends, tomatoes with herbs, and canned soups let you get a head start.

Stocking Your Pantry

The key to pulling off a terrific meal on short notice (and preventing an unexpected grocery run) is to have a well-stocked pantry. If you cover your bases, you'll always have things in the cupboard that will work well together. Here are some suggestions for basic ingredients to keep on hand.

3. USE MIXES IN NEW WAYS. A cake mix can be a good basis for cookies or bars. Biscuit and cookie mixes can also provide inspiration for a new recipe.

4. CHECK OUT PREPARED FOODS. Just because food is already prepared doesn't mean you need to serve it as is! Pre-cut fruit and veggies from the salad bar, rotisserie chicken from the deli—use these as starting points for your own dishes.

5. MAKE CONVENIENCE PRODUCTS YOUR OWN. Rice, stuffing and pasta mixes are ideal for experimentation. Try adding chopped fresh apple, celery and onion to a stuffing mix, for example, or add shrimp to a rice mix. Take a second look at convenience breads, such as crescent rolls, biscuits and frozen bread dough. You don't have to make bread with them—they also work with some well-chosen ingredients to make appetizers, casseroles or calzones.

Stock, broth or bouillon • vinegar • eggs • milk • condensed soups • salsa • flour • herbs and spices • lemons • garlic • pastas • ramen • tomato sauce and paste • canned tomatoes • canned beans• canned tuna • bread or rolls • rice mixes • onions • shredded cheeses • butter • frozen vegetables • prepared salad dressings • olives • honey • hot sauce • bread crumbs • prepared mustard • bacon • frozen bread dough • frozen fruit • ground beef • shredded cooked chicken • frozen shrimp or scallops • smoked sausages

BREAKFAST

UPSIDE-DOWN BACON PANCAKE
P. 33

1

2

3

4

5

DIG INTO DOZENS OF WINNING WAYS TO LOVE
THE MOST IMPORTANT MEAL OF THE DAY!

ORANGE-GLAZED BACON

ORANGE-GLAZED BACON

Just when you thought bacon couldn't get any tastier, we whipped up this recipe starring the favorite breakfast meat drizzled with a sweet orange glaze.
—*Taste of Home* Test Kitchen

- - - - - - - - - - - - - - - - - - - -

Prep: 20 min. • **Bake:** 25 min.
Makes: 8 servings

- ¾ cup orange juice
- ¼ cup honey
- 1 Tbsp. Dijon mustard
- ¼ tsp. ground ginger
- ⅛ tsp. pepper
- 1 lb. bacon strips

1. In a small saucepan, combine the first 5 ingredients. Bring to a boil; cook until liquid is reduced to ⅓ cup.
2. Preheat oven to 350°. Place the bacon on a rack in an ungreased 15x10x1-in. baking pan. Bake bacon for 10 minutes; drain.
3. Drizzle half of glaze over bacon. Bake for 10 minutes. Turn bacon and drizzle with remaining glaze. Bake until golden brown, 5-10 minutes longer. Place bacon on waxed paper until set. Serve warm.
3 glazed bacon strips: 146 cal., 8g fat (3g sat. fat), 21mg chol., 407mg sod., 12g carb. (11g sugars, 0 fiber), 7g pro.

CREAMY BAKED EGGS

This recipe is so simple, and the eggs come out just as my husband likes them every time. If you like soft yolks, cook eggs for 9 minutes; for firmer yolks, cook for about 11 minutes.
—Macey Allen, Green Forest, AR

- - - - - - - - - - - - - - - - - - - -

Takes: 25 min. • **Makes:** 8 servings

- ¼ cup half-and-half cream
- 8 large eggs
- 1 cup shredded Jarlsberg cheese
- 2 Tbsp. grated Parmesan cheese
- ¼ tsp. salt
- ⅛ tsp. pepper
- 2 green onions, chopped

1. Preheat oven to 400°. Pour the cream into a greased cast-iron or other ovenproof skillet. Gently break an egg into a small bowl; slip the egg into the skillet. Repeat with the rest of the eggs. Sprinkle with cheeses, salt and pepper.
2. Bake until the egg whites are completely set and yolks begin to thicken but are not hard, 10-12 minutes. Top with green onions; serve immediately.
1 baked egg: 135 cal., 9g fat (4g sat. fat), 200mg chol., 237mg sod., 2g carb. (1g sugars, 0 fiber), 11g pro.

CREAMY BAKED EGGS

SIMPLE CINNAMON ROLLS

Refrigerated crescent roll dough makes it a snap to whip up these oven-fresh goodies. The glaze has a hint of orange.

—*Taste of Home* Test Kitchen

Takes: 20 min. • **Makes:** 4 rolls

- 1   **tube (4 oz.) refrigerated crescent rolls**
- 1   **Tbsp. sugar**
- ⅛   **tsp. ground cinnamon**
- ¼   **cup confectioners' sugar**
- 1¼ **tsp. orange juice**

1. Preheat oven to 375°. Unroll crescent dough into 1 rectangle; seal perforations. Combine sugar and cinnamon; sprinkle over dough. Roll up jelly-roll style, starting with a short side; pinch seam to seal. Using a serrated knife, cut into 4 slices.

2. Place rolls, pinched side down, in ungreased muffin cups. Bake for 10-12 minutes or until golden brown. Cool for 5 minutes before removing from pan to a wire rack. In a small bowl, combine confectioners' sugar and orange juice; drizzle over the still-warm rolls.

1 roll: 154 cal., 6g fat (2g sat. fat), 0 chol., 223mg sod., 22g carb. (12g sugars, 0 fiber), 2g pro.

PEANUT BUTTER & JELLY OVERNIGHT OATS

This yummy breakfast bowl gives everyone's favorite sandwich a healthy twist. Switch to crunchy peanut butter and sprinkle some chopped peanuts over the top if you like extra crunch.

—*Taste of Home* Test Kitchen

Prep: 10 min. + chilling
Makes: 4 servings

- ¼   **cup creamy peanut butter**
- 2   **Tbsp. honey**
- 1½ **cups 2% milk**
- 1⅓ **cups old-fashioned oats**
- ¼   **cup strawberry jelly**

1. In a small bowl, beat peanut butter and honey until smooth. Gradually add the milk until combined. Add the oats and mix to combine. Chill in refrigerator, covered, overnight.

2. Whisk the jelly slightly and swirl 1 Tbsp. into each serving.

1 serving: 323 cal., 12g fat (3g sat. fat), 7mg chol., 112mg sod., 48g carb. (27g sugars, 3g fiber), 10g pro.

PEANUT BUTTER & JELLY OVERNIGHT OATS

GERMAN POTATO
OMELET

GERMAN POTATO OMELET

This is an old German dish that all of us kids enjoyed when we were growing up. With a side of toast and jam, this flavorful omelet is sure to make your family as happy as it made all of us.

—Katherine Stallwood, Richland, WA

- -

Takes: 30 min. • **Makes:** 4 servings

- 2 **large potatoes, thinly sliced**
- ¼ **cup butter, divided**
- ½ **cup sliced green onions**
- 8 **large eggs**
- ¼ **cup 2% milk**
  Salt and pepper to taste

1. In a large skillet, cook potatoes in 2 Tbsp. butter for 15 minutes or until browned and tender. Sprinkle potatoes with onions; set aside and keep warm.

2. In a large nonstick skillet, melt remaining butter over medium-high heat. Whisk the eggs and milk. Add egg mixture to skillet (mixture should set immediately at edges).

3. As eggs set, push cooked edges toward the center, letting uncooked portion flow underneath. When the eggs are set, spoon potato mixture on 1 side; fold other side over the filling. Invert omelet onto a plate to serve. Cut into wedges and season as desired.

1 piece: 400 cal., 22g fat (11g sat. fat), 404mg chol., 253mg sod., 35g carb. (3g sugars, 4g fiber), 17g pro.

SAUSAGE & CRESCENT ROLL CASSEROLE

SAUSAGE & CRESCENT ROLL CASSEROLE

I made this tasty brunch casserole for a baby shower. It saved the day: Preparing it ahead gave me more time to finish decorating for the party.
—Melody Craft, Conroe, TX

Prep: 15 min. • **Bake:** 35 min.
Makes: 12 servings

- 1   lb. bulk pork sausage
- 1   tube (8 oz.) refrigerated crescent rolls
- 2   cups shredded part-skim mozzarella cheese
- 8   large eggs
- 2   cups 2% milk
- ½   tsp. salt
- ¼   tsp. pepper

1. Preheat oven to 375°. In a large skillet, cook sausage over medium heat 6-8 minutes or until no longer pink, breaking into crumbles; drain. Unroll the crescent roll dough into a greased 13x9-in. baking dish. Seal seams and perforations. Sprinkle with sausage and cheese.
2. Whisk eggs, milk, salt and pepper; pour over sausage and cheese.
3. Bake, uncovered, 35-40 minutes or until a knife inserted in the center comes out clean. Let casserole stand 5-10 minutes before serving.
To make ahead: Refrigerate unbaked casserole, covered, several hours or overnight. To use, preheat oven to 375°. Remove casserole from the refrigerator while oven heats. Bake as directed, increasing the time as necessary until a knife inserted in the center comes out clean. Let stand 5-10 minutes before serving.
1 piece: 283 cal., 19g fat (6g sat. fat), 160mg chol., 662mg sod., 12g carb. (4g sugars, 0 fiber), 15g pro.

TROPICAL BERRY SMOOTHIES

This fruity, healthy smoothie is a big hit with kids and adults alike because it tastes like a treat and still delivers the vitamins. The recipe is easy to increase based on the number of people you'll be serving.

—Hillary Engler, Cape Girardeau, MO

- -

Takes: 10 min. • **Makes:** 2 servings

- 1   **cup pina colada juice blend**
- 1   **container (6 oz.) vanilla yogurt**
- ⅓   **cup frozen unsweetened strawberries**
- ¼   **cup frozen mango chunks**
- ¼   **cup frozen unsweetened blueberries**

In a blender, combine all ingredients; cover and process for 30 seconds or until smooth. Pour into chilled glasses; serve immediately.

1¼ cups: 172 cal., 2g fat (1g sat. fat), 4mg chol., 62mg sod., 35g carb. (32g sugars, 2g fiber), 5g pro.

TROPICAL BERRY SMOOTHIES

MEDITERRANEAN OMELET

BACON & EGG GRAVY

My husband, Ron, created this wonderful breakfast gravy. It's home-style and old-fashioned. It's a great breakfast with fruit salad on the side.

—Terry Bray, Winter Haven, FL

- -

Takes: 20 min. • **Makes:** 2 servings

- 6   bacon strips, diced
- 5   Tbsp. all-purpose flour
- 1½ cups water
- 1   can (12 oz.) evaporated milk
- 3   hard-boiled large eggs, sliced
     Salt and pepper to taste
- 4   slices bread, toasted

In a skillet, cook bacon over medium heat until crisp; remove to paper towels. Stir flour into the drippings until blended; cook over medium heat until the mixture is browned, stirring constantly. Gradually add the water and milk. Bring to a boil; cook and stir for 2 minutes or until thickened. Add bacon, eggs, salt and pepper. Serve over toast.

1 serving: 934 cal., 61g fat (26g sat. fat), 424mg chol., 1030mg sod., 58g carb. (21g sugars, 2g fiber), 33g pro.

★ ★ ★ ★ ★ **READER REVIEW**

"Great recipe reminiscent of one from my youth. Good for breakfast, lunch or dinner. Excellent over hot biscuits, grits or rice, too."

—OWLTREE, TASTEOFHOME.COM

MEDITERRANEAN OMELET

This fluffy omelet gives us reason to get a move on for breakfast. For a bit of extra flair, add some chopped fresh herbs like basil, oregano or tarragon.

—Milynne Charlton, Scarborough, ON

- -

Takes: 10 min. • **Makes:** 2 servings

- 4   large eggs
- ¼   cup water
- ⅛   tsp. salt
     Dash pepper
- 1   Tbsp. butter
- ¼   cup crumbled feta or goat cheese
- ¼   cup chopped tomato
- 1   green onion, chopped

1. In a small bowl, whisk eggs, water, salt and pepper until blended. In a large nonstick skillet, heat butter over medium-high heat. Pour in egg mixture. Mixture should set immediately at edge. As eggs set, push cooked portions toward the center, letting the uncooked eggs flow underneath.

2. When eggs are thickened and no liquid egg remains, add cheese, tomato and green onion to 1 side. Fold omelet in half and cut into 2 portions; slide onto plates.

½ omelet: 236 cal., 18g fat (8g sat. fat), 395mg chol., 472mg sod., 3g carb. (1g sugars, 1g fiber), 15g pro.

BACON & EGG GRAVY

BREAKFAST WRAPS

BREAKFAST WRAPS

We like quick and simple morning meals during the week, and these wraps can be prepped ahead of time. With just a minute in the microwave, breakfast is ready to go.
—Betty Kleberger, Florissant, MO

- -

Takes: 15 min. • **Makes:** 4 servings

- 6 large eggs
- 2 Tbsp. 2% milk
- ¼ tsp. pepper
- 1 Tbsp. canola oil
- 1 cup shredded cheddar cheese

¾ cup diced fully cooked ham
4 flour tortillas (8 in.), warmed

1. In a small bowl, whisk the eggs, milk and pepper. In a large skillet, heat oil. Add egg mixture; cook and stir over medium heat until eggs are completely set. Stir in the cheese and ham.

2. Spoon egg mixture down the center of each tortilla; roll up.

Freeze option: Wrap cooled egg wrap in foil and freeze in a freezer container. To use, thaw in refrigerator overnight. Remove foil; wrap tortilla in a moist paper towel. Microwave on high until wrap is heated through, 30-60 seconds. Serve immediately.

1 serving: 436 cal., 24g fat (10g sat. fat), 364mg chol., 853mg sod., 28g carb. (1g sugars, 0 fiber), 25g pro.

Pizza Breakfast Wraps: Prepare recipe as directed, replacing cheddar cheese and ham with mozzarella cheese and cooked sausage. Serve with warm marinara sauce on the side.

Pulled Pork Breakfast Wraps: Prepare recipe as directed, replacing cheddar cheese and ham with smoked Gouda cheese and precooked pulled pork. Serve with warm barbecue sauce on the side.

PORK SAUSAGE PATTIES

Savory pork sausage patties will give any breakfast a boost. These little beauties will have everyone coming back for seconds.

—Carole Thomson, Komarno, MB

- -

Takes: 25 min. • **Makes:** 6 servings

1	large egg, beaten
⅓	cup 2% milk
½	cup chopped onion
2	Tbsp. all-purpose flour
⅛	tsp. salt
	Dash pepper
1	lb. sage bulk pork sausage

1. In a large bowl, combine first 6 ingredients. Crumble sausage over mixture and mix lightly but thoroughly. Shape into 6 patties.

2. In a large skillet, cook patties over medium heat for 6 minutes on each side or until meat is no longer pink, turning occasionally.

Freeze option: Prepare uncooked patties and freeze them, covered, on a foil-lined baking sheet until firm. Transfer patties to a freezer container; return to freezer. To use, cook frozen patties as directed, increasing time as necessary for a thermometer to read 160°.

1 patty: 219 cal., 18g fat (6g sat. fat), 73mg chol., 527mg sod., 5g carb. (1g sugars, 0 fiber), 10g pro.

CUBAN BREAKFAST SANDWICHES

Grab hold of breakfast time by serving these warm energy-boosting sandwiches. They travel well on hectic mornings, and the hearty helping of protein will help keep hunger at bay.

—Lacie Griffin, Austin, TX

- -

Takes: 20 min. • **Makes:** 4 servings

1	loaf (1 lb.) Cuban or French bread
4	large eggs
16	pieces thinly sliced hard salami
8	slices deli ham
8	slices Swiss cheese

1. Split bread in half lengthwise; cut into 4 pieces. In a large skillet coated with cooking spray, fry eggs until yolks are set. Layer bread bottoms with salami, ham, egg and cheese; replace tops.

2. Cook on a panini maker or indoor grill for 2 minutes or until bread is browned and cheese is melted.

1 sandwich: 697 cal., 29g fat (12g sat. fat), 280mg chol., 1949mg sod., 61g carb. (1g sugars, 3g fiber), 43g pro.

TEST KITCHEN TIP
Cuban bread, a white yeast bread traditionally made with lard, can be hard to find. Any sliced yeast bread or bakery sandwich rolls will work in this recipe.

PORK SAUSAGE PATTIES

PEANUT BUTTER BANANA OVERNIGHT OATS

PEANUT BUTTER BANANA OVERNIGHT OATS

Talk about wholesome and quick! You'll be satisfied right up until lunchtime with these peanut butter banana overnight oats.
—*Taste of Home* Test Kitchen

Prep: 10 min. + chilling
Makes: 1 serving

⅓   cup old-fashioned oats
¼   cup mashed ripe banana
3   Tbsp. fat-free milk
1   Tbsp. honey
1   Tbsp. creamy peanut butter, warmed
      Optional: Sliced ripe banana and honey

In a small container or Mason jar, combine oats, banana, milk, honey and peanut butter. Seal; refrigerate overnight. If desired, top with sliced bananas and drizzle with honey.
1 serving: 325 cal., 10g fat (2g sat. fat), 1mg chol., 89mg sod., 54g carb. (29g sugars, 5g fiber), 9g pro.

BACON BREAKFAST CASSEROLE

BACON BREAKFAST CASSEROLE

This easy breakfast dish allows me to make a comforting family favorite that doesn't take a lot of prep. It's also great for big brunch gatherings.
—Paula Lawson, Springfield, OH

- -

Prep: 30 min.
Cook: 4 hours + standing
Makes: 12 servings

- 1   lb. bacon strips, chopped
- 1   pkg. (28 oz.) frozen potatoes O'Brien, thawed
- 3   cups shredded Mexican cheese blend
- 12   large eggs
- 1   cup 2% milk
- ½   tsp. salt
- ½   tsp. pepper
       Minced fresh parsley, optional

1. In a large skillet, cook bacon in batches over medium heat until crisp. Remove to paper towels to drain.

2. In a greased 4- or 5-qt. slow cooker, layer a third of each of the following: potatoes, bacon and cheese. Repeat layers twice. In a large bowl, whisk eggs, milk, salt and pepper; pour over top. Cook, covered, on low until eggs are set, 4-5 hours. Turn off slow cooker. Remove crock insert to a wire rack; let stand, uncovered, 30 minutes before serving. If desired, sprinkle with parsley.

1 serving: 306 cal., 19g fat (8g sat. fat), 226mg chol., 606mg sod., 13g carb. (2g sugars, 2g fiber), 18g pro.

3. To serve, cut each omelet into 3 wedges; place each wedge on a roll. Add tomatoes and, if desired, ketchup, onion and pickles.

2 sliders: 507 cal., 23g fat (9g sat. fat), 348mg chol., 1032mg sod., 39g carb. (5g sugars, 3g fiber), 34g pro.

SAUSAGE BACON BITES

These tasty morsels are perfect with almost any egg dish or as finger foods that party guests can just pop into their mouths.
—Pat Waymire, Yellow Springs, OH

- -

Prep: 20 min. + chilling
Bake: 35 min.
Makes: about 3½ dozen

- ¾ lb. sliced bacon
- 2 pkg. (8 oz. each) frozen fully cooked breakfast sausage links, thawed
- ½ cup plus 2 Tbsp. packed brown sugar, divided

1. Cut bacon strips widthwise in half; cut sausage links in half. Wrap a piece of bacon around each piece of sausage. Place ½ cup brown sugar in a shallow bowl; roll the wrapped sausages in sugar. Secure each with a toothpick. Place in a foil-lined 15x10x1-in. baking pan. Cover and refrigerate wrapped sausages 4 hours or overnight.

2. Preheat oven to 350°. Sprinkle wrapped sausages with 1 Tbsp. brown sugar. Bake them until bacon is crisp, 35-40 minutes, turning once. Sprinkle bacon with remaining brown sugar.

1 piece: 51 cal., 4g fat (1g sat. fat), 6mg chol., 100mg sod., 4g carb. (4g sugars, 0 fiber), 2g pro.

CHEESEBURGER OMELET SLIDERS

CHEESEBURGER OMELET SLIDERS

A cheeseburger inside an omelet? Yes, please! This fun twist on two breakfast and dinner faves is easy to assemble and delicious any time of day.
—Denise LaRoche, Hudson, NH

- -

Prep: 25 min. • **Cook:** 25 min.
Makes: 6 servings

- 1 lb. lean ground beef (90% lean)
- 1 tsp. salt, divided
- ½ tsp. pepper, divided
- 8 large eggs
- ½ cup water
- 1 cup shredded Havarti cheese
- 12 dinner rolls, split
- 12 tomato slices
  Optional: Ketchup, onion slices and pickle slices

1. Combine beef, ½ tsp. salt and ¼ tsp. pepper; mix lightly but thoroughly. Shape into twelve 2-in. patties. In a large skillet, cook burgers over medium heat until cooked through, 2-3 minutes per side. Remove from heat; keep warm.

2. Whisk together eggs, water and the remaining salt and pepper. Place a small nonstick skillet, lightly oiled, over medium-high heat; pour in ½ cup egg mixture. Mixture should set immediately at edges. As eggs set, push cooked edges toward the center, letting uncooked eggs flow underneath. When the eggs are thickened and no liquid egg remains, sprinkle ⅓ cup cheese on 1 half. Top cheese with 3 burgers, spacing them evenly; fold the omelet in half. Slide onto a cutting board; tent with foil to keep warm. Repeat to make 3 more omelets.

SAUSAGE
BACON BITES

CHERRY SYRUP

My mom and grandma have been making this fruity syrup to serve with fluffy waffles and pancakes ever since I was a little girl. Now I make it for my sons, who love it as much as I do!

—Sandra Harrington, Nipomo, CA

- -

Takes: 30 min. • **Makes:** 3 cups

- 1 pkg. (12 oz.) frozen pitted dark sweet cherries, thawed
- 1 cup water
- 2½ cups sugar
- 2 Tbsp. butter
- ½ tsp. almond extract
   Dash ground cinnamon

1. Bring cherries and water to a boil in a small saucepan. Reduce heat; simmer, uncovered, for 20 minutes.
2. Add sugar and butter; cook and stir until sugar is dissolved. Remove from the heat; stir in the almond extract and cinnamon.
3. Cool leftovers; transfer to airtight containers. Store in the refrigerator for up to 2 weeks.
2 Tbsp.: 100 cal., 1g fat (1g sat. fat), 3mg chol., 7mg sod., 23g carb. (23g sugars, 0 fiber), 0 pro.

DID YOU KNOW?

Cinnamon comes in two basic types: Ceylon and cassia. Ceylon cinnamon's delicate, complex flavor is ideal for ice creams and dessert sauces. The spicy, bolder cassia cinnamon (often labeled simply as cinnamon) is preferred for baking.

SPARKLING PEACH BELLINIS

Folks will savor the subtle kiss of peach flavor in this elegant brunch beverage.

—*Taste of Home* Test Kitchen

- -

Prep: 35 min. + cooling
Makes: 12 servings

- 3 medium peaches, halved
- 1 Tbsp. honey
- 1 can (11.3 oz.) peach nectar, chilled
- 2 bottles (750 ml each) champagne or sparkling grape juice, chilled

1. Preheat oven to 375°. Line a baking sheet with a large piece of heavy-duty foil (about 18x12 in.). Place peach halves, cut sides up, on foil; drizzle with honey. Fold foil over peaches and seal.
2. Bake for 25-30 minutes or until tender. Cool completely; remove and discard the peels. In a food processor, process until smooth.
3. Transfer peach puree to a pitcher. Add the nectar and 1 bottle of champagne; stir until combined. Pour into 12 champagne flutes or wine glasses; top with remaining champagne. Serve immediately.
¾ cup: 74 cal., 0 fat (0 sat. fat), 0 chol., 2mg sod., 9g carb. (7g sugars, 1g fiber), 0 pro.

SPARKLING PEACH BELLINIS

FRESH CORN
OMELET

FRESH CORN OMELET

I throw in homegrown corn and from-scratch salsa when I make this super summertime omelet. Sprinkle in onions, mushrooms, peppers and breakfast meat to customize it.

—William Stone, Robson, WV

- -

Takes: 25 min. • **Makes:** 4 servings

- 10 **large eggs**
- 2 **Tbsp. water**
- ¼ **tsp. salt**
- ¼ **tsp. pepper**

- 2 **tsp. plus 2 Tbsp. butter, divided**
- 1 **cup fresh or frozen corn, thawed**
- ½ **cup shredded cheddar cheese**
  Fresh salsa

1. In a small bowl, whisk the eggs, water, salt and pepper until blended. In a large nonstick skillet, heat 2 tsp. butter over medium heat. Add corn; cook and stir 1-2 minutes or until tender. Remove from pan.

2. In same pan, heat 1 Tbsp. butter over medium-high heat. Pour in half of the egg mixture. Mixture should set immediately at edges. As eggs set, push cooked portions toward the center, letting uncooked eggs flow underneath. When eggs are thickened and no liquid egg remains, spoon half of the corn on 1 side of the eggs; sprinkle with ¼ cup cheese. Fold omelet in half. Cut in half; slide each half onto a plate.

3. Repeat with remaining butter, egg mixture and filling. Serve with salsa.

½ omelet: 336 cal., 25g fat (12g sat. fat), 500mg chol., 482mg sod., 8g carb. (3g sugars, 1g fiber), 20g pro.

BREAKFAST BREAD BOWLS

BREAKFAST BREAD BOWLS

These bread bowls are so tasty, simple and elegant, you'll wonder why you haven't been making them for years. My wife loves when I make these for her in the morning.

—Patrick Lavin Jr., Birdsboro, PA

- -

Prep: 20 min. • **Bake:** 20 min.
Makes: 4 servings

½ cup chopped pancetta
4 crusty hard rolls (4 in. wide)
½ cup finely chopped
   fresh mushrooms
4 large eggs
⅛ tsp. salt
⅛ tsp. pepper
¼ cup shredded Gruyere or
   fontina cheese

1. Preheat oven to 350°. In a small skillet, cook pancetta over medium heat until meat is browned, stirring occasionally. Remove with a slotted spoon; drain on paper towels.
2. Meanwhile, cut a thin slice off top of each roll. Hollow out bottom of roll, leaving a ½-in.-thick shell (save removed bread for another use); place shells on an ungreased baking sheet.
3. Add mushrooms and pancetta to bread shells. Carefully break an egg into each; sprinkle eggs with salt and pepper. Sprinkle with cheese. Bake 18-22 minutes or until egg whites are completely set and yolks begin to thicken but are not hard.

1 breakfast bowl: 256 cal., 13g fat (5g sat. fat), 206mg chol., 658mg sod., 19g carb. (1g sugars, 1g fiber), 14g pro.

TURKEY BREAKFAST SAUSAGE

These hearty sausage patties are loaded with flavor but have a fraction of the sodium and fat found in commercial breakfast sausage links.

—Judy Culbertson, Dansville, NY

- -

Takes: 20 min. • **Makes:** 8 servings

- 1 lb. lean ground turkey
- ¾ tsp. salt
- ½ tsp. rubbed sage
- ½ tsp. pepper
- ¼ tsp. ground ginger

1. Crumble turkey into a large bowl. Add salt, sage, pepper and ginger; mix lightly but thoroughly. Shape into eight 2-in. patties.

2. In a greased cast-iron or other heavy skillet, cook the patties over medium heat until a thermometer reads 165° and the juices run clear, 4-6 minutes on each side.

1 patty: 85 cal., 5g fat (1g sat. fat), 45mg chol., 275mg sod., 0 carb. (0 sugars, 0 fiber), 10g pro. **Diabetic exchanges:** 1 lean meat, ½ fat.

TURKEY BREAKFAST SAUSAGE

CINNAMON APPLESAUCE PANCAKES

CHEESY HASH BROWN BAKE

Prepare this cheesy dish ahead of time for less stress on brunch day. You'll love it!
—Karen Burns, Chandler, TX

- -

Prep: 10 min. • **Bake:** 40 min.
Makes: 10 servings

- 1 pkg. (30 oz.) frozen shredded hash brown potatoes, thawed
- 2 cans (10¾ oz. each) condensed cream of potato soup, undiluted
- 2 cups sour cream
- 2 cups shredded cheddar cheese, divided
- 1 cup grated Parmesan cheese

1. Preheat oven to 350°. In a large bowl, combine the potatoes, soup, sour cream, 1¾ cups cheddar and the Parmesan. Place in a greased 3-qt. baking dish. Top with the remaining cheddar cheese.
2. Bake, uncovered, until bubbly and cheese is melted, 40-45 minutes. Let stand 5 minutes before serving.
½ cup: 305 cal., 18g fat (12g sat. fat), 65mg chol., 554mg sod., 21g carb. (3g sugars, 1g fiber), 12g pro.

★ ★ ★ ★ ★ **READER REVIEW**
"This is the first thing I made from scratch in decades and it turned out wonderfully! Everyone loved it! Next time I'm going to add bacon bits."
—JIMWATTSR, TASTEOFHOME.COM

CINNAMON APPLESAUCE PANCAKES

These fluffy, tender pancakes are so good, you just might skip the syrup. They were created for Christmas morning but have since wowed folks at church breakfasts as well as gatherings with family and friends. The cinnamon is a delightful touch. Kids love to gobble them up!
—Richard DeVore, Gibsonburg, OH

- -

Takes: 20 min. • **Makes:** 3 servings

- 1 cup complete buttermilk pancake mix
- 1 tsp. ground cinnamon
- 1 cup chunky cinnamon applesauce
- ¼ cup water
  Maple syrup and butter

1. Combine pancake mix and cinnamon. Add applesauce and water; stir just until moistened.
2. Pour batter by ¼ cupfuls onto a greased hot griddle; turn cakes when bubbles form on top. Cook until the second side is golden brown. Serve with syrup and butter.
3 pancakes: 218 cal., 2g fat (0 sat. fat), 0 chol., 649mg sod., 50g carb. (18g sugars, 2g fiber), 3g pro.

CHEESY
HASH BROWN
BAKE

SAUSAGE CHEESE PUFFS

SAUSAGE CHEESE PUFFS

People are always surprised when I tell them there are only four ingredients in these tasty bite-sized puffs. Cheesy and spicy, the golden bites are a fun novelty at brunch, and they also make yummy party appetizers.
—Della Moore, Troy, NY

- -

Takes: 25 min.
Makes: about 4 dozen

1 lb. bulk Italian sausage
3 cups biscuit/baking mix
4 cups shredded cheddar
   cheese
¾ cup water

1. Preheat oven to 400°. In a large skillet, cook sausage over medium heat until meat is no longer pink, 5-7 minutes, break sausage into crumbles; drain.

2. In a large bowl, combine biscuit mix and cheese; stir in the sausage. Add water and toss with a fork until moistened. Shape the dough into 1½-in. balls. Place 2 in. apart on ungreased baking sheets.

3. Bake until puffed and golden brown, 12-15 minutes. Cool on wire racks.

1 puff: 89 cal., 6g fat (3g sat. fat), 14mg chol., 197mg sod., 6g carb. (0 sugars, 0 fiber), 4g pro.

MAKE-AHEAD EGGS BENEDICT TOAST CUPS

When I was growing up, we had a family tradition of having eggs Benedict with champagne and orange juice for our Christmas breakfast. But now that I'm cooking, a fussy breakfast isn't my style. I wanted to come up with a dish I could make ahead that would mimic the flavors of traditional eggs Benedict and would also freeze well.

—Lyndsay Wells, Ladysmith, BC

- -

Prep: 30 min. • **Bake:** 10 min.
Makes: 1 dozen

6   English muffins, split
1   envelope hollandaise sauce mix
12 slices Canadian bacon, quartered
1   tsp. pepper
1   Tbsp. olive oil
6   large eggs
1   Tbsp. butter

1. Preheat oven to 375°. Flatten muffin halves with a rolling pin; press into greased muffin cups. Bake until lightly browned, about 10 minutes.

2. Meanwhile, prepare hollandaise sauce according to the package directions; cool slightly. Sprinkle bacon with pepper. In a large skillet, cook bacon in oil over medium heat until partially cooked but not crisp. Remove to paper towels to drain. Divide bacon among muffin cups. Wipe skillet clean.

3. Whisk eggs and ½ cup cooled hollandaise sauce until blended. In the skillet, heat butter over medium heat. Pour in egg mixture; cook and stir until eggs are thickened and no liquid egg remains. Divide the egg mixture among muffin cups; top with remaining hollandaise sauce.

4. Bake until heated through, 8-10 minutes. Serve warm.

Overnight option: Refrigerate the unbaked cups, covered, overnight. Bake until golden brown, 10-12 minutes.

Freeze option: Cover and freeze unbaked cups in muffin cups until firm. Transfer to an airtight container; return to freezer. To use, bake cups in muffin tin as directed, increasing time to 25-30 minutes. Cover the cups loosely with foil if necessary to prevent overbrowning.

1 toast cup: 199 cal., 11g fat (5g sat. fat), 114mg chol., 495mg sod., 15g carb. (2g sugars, 1g fiber), 9g pro.

★ ★ ★ ★ ★ **READER REVIEW**

"We LOVE this recipe! So yummy and easy to make! The English muffins are a little tricky to roll out and press in, but it is worth the extra effort."

— KYMBERLYFLEWELLING, TASTEOFHOME.COM

MAKE-AHEAD EGGS BENEDICT TOAST CUPS

ZIPPY PRALINE BACON

I'm always looking for recipes to enhance the usual eggs and bacon. My husband came home from a brunch raving about this one, and the hostess shared the recipe. Just be sure to make more than you think you might need because everybody will definitely want seconds!
—Myrt Pfannkuche, Pell City, AL

- -

Takes: 20 min. • **Makes:** 20 pieces

1	lb. bacon strips
3	Tbsp. brown sugar
1½	tsp. chili powder
¼	cup finely chopped pecans

1. Preheat oven to 425°. Arrange bacon in a single layer in 2 foil-lined 15x10x1-in. pans. Bake 10 minutes; carefully pour off drippings.

2. Mix brown sugar and chili powder; sprinkle over bacon. Sprinkle with pecans. Bake until bacon is crisp, 5-10 minutes. Drain on paper towels.

1 strip: 58 cal., 4g fat (1g sat. fat), 8mg chol., 151mg sod., 2g carb. (2g sugars, 0 fiber), 3g pro.

**ZIPPY PRALINE
BACON**

**EGG-TOPPED
BISCUIT WAFFLES**

EGG-TOPPED
BISCUIT WAFFLES

*Breakfast for dinner is always
a hit at our house. As a mom,
I enjoy transforming a basic
breakfast sandwich into one
that's magical and kid-friendly.*
—Amy Lents, Grand Forks, ND

- -

Takes: 25 min. • **Makes:** 4 waffles

1½ **cups biscuit/baking mix**
¾ **cup shredded Swiss cheese**
⅛ **tsp. pepper**
½ **cup 2% milk**
4 **large eggs**

4 **bacon strips,
cooked and crumbled
Optional: Cubed avocado and
pico de gallo**

1. Preheat a 4-square waffle maker.
Place baking mix, cheese and pepper
in a bowl. Add milk; stir just until
moistened. Transfer to a lightly
floured surface; knead dough gently
4 to 6 times. Pat or roll the dough
into an 8-in. square; cut into four
4-in. squares.

2. Generously grease top and
bottom grids of waffle maker. Place
1 portion of dough on each section
of the waffle maker, pressing an
indentation in each for eggs.

3. Break an egg over each biscuit;
sprinkle with bacon. Close the lid
carefully over eggs; bake according
to manufacturer's directions until
biscuits are golden brown. If desired,
top with avocado and pico de gallo.

1 serving: 386 cal., 20g fat (8g sat.
fat), 215mg chol., 802mg sod., 33g
carb. (3g sugars, 1g fiber), 19g pro.

**UPSIDE-DOWN
BACON PANCAKE**

UPSIDE-DOWN BACON PANCAKE

Make a big impression when you present one family-size bacon pancake. The brown sugar adds sweetness that complements the salty bacon. If you can fit extra bacon in the skillet and want to add more, go for it.
—Mindie Hilton, Susanville, CA

- -

Prep: 10 min.
Bake: 20 min. + cooling
Makes: 6 servings

6   bacon strips, coarsely chopped
¼   cup packed brown sugar
2   cups complete buttermilk pancake mix
1½ cups water
    Optional: Maple syrup and butter

1. In a large cast-iron or other ovenproof skillet, cook bacon over medium heat until crisp. Remove bacon to paper towels with a slotted spoon. Remove drippings, reserving 2 Tbsp. Return bacon to pan with reserved drippings; sprinkle with brown sugar.

2. In a small bowl, combine pancake mix and water just until moistened. Pour into pan.

3. Bake at 350° until a toothpick inserted in the center comes out clean, 18-20 minutes. Cool for 10 minutes before inverting onto a serving plate. Serve warm, with maple syrup and butter as desired.

1 piece: 265 cal., 9g fat (3g sat. fat), 12mg chol., 802mg sod., 41g carb. (13g sugars, 1g fiber), 6g pro.

CALIFORNIA DREAM SMOOTHIE

CALIFORNIA DREAM SMOOTHIE

It's sunshine in a smoothie! This one's a true California treat—sweet and tangy from start to finish.
—Sonya Labbe, West Hollywood, CA

- -

Takes: 15 min. • **Makes:** 5 servings

2   cups ice cubes
1   can (12 oz.) frozen orange juice concentrate, thawed
1   cup 2% milk
1   cup vanilla yogurt
½   cup honey

Pulse all ingredients in a blender until smooth. Serve immediately.

1 cup: 269 cal., 2g fat (1g sat. fat), 6mg chol., 61mg sod., 61g carb. (57g sugars, 1g fiber), 6g pro.

TEST KITCHEN TIP
For easy cleanup, spritz the measuring cup with cooking spray before measuring sticky ingredients like honey.

SNACKS & APPETIZERS

**GARLIC-HERB
MINI QUICHES P. 56**

1

2

3

4

5

WHETHER YOU'RE FEEDING A CROWD OR IN NEED OF
A PICK-ME-UP SNACK, YOU'LL FIND THE ANSWER HERE.

SPINACH & TURKEY PINWHEELS

STICKY HONEY CHICKEN WINGS

This honey chicken wings recipe was given to me by a special lady who was like a grandmother to me.

—Marisa Raponi, Vaughan, ON

- -

Prep: 15 min. + marinating
Bake: 30 min. • **Makes:** 3 dozen

- ½   cup orange blossom honey
- ⅓   cup white vinegar
- 2   Tbsp. paprika
- 2   tsp. salt
- 1   tsp. pepper
- 4   lbs. chicken wings

1. Combine honey, vinegar, paprika, salt and pepper in a small bowl.
2. Cut through the 2 wing joints with a sharp knife, discarding wing tips. Add the remaining wing pieces and honey mixture to a large bowl; stir to coat. Cover and refrigerate 4 hours or overnight.
3. Preheat oven to 375°. Remove wings; reserve honey mixture. Place wings on greased 15x10x1-in. baking pans. Bake until the juices run clear, about 30 minutes, turning the wings halfway through.
4. Meanwhile, place reserved honey mixture in a small saucepan. Bring to a boil; cook 1 minute.
5. Remove wings from oven; preheat broiler. Place wings on a greased rack in a broiler pan; brush with the honey mixture. Broil 4-5 in. from heat until crispy, 3-5 minutes. Serve with remaining honey mixture.
1 piece: 71 cal., 4g fat (1g sat. fat), 16mg chol., 147mg sod., 4g carb. (4g sugars, 0 fiber), 5g pro.

SPINACH & TURKEY PINWHEELS

Need an awesome snack for game day? My kids love these quick and easy four-ingredient turkey pinwheels. Go ahead and make them the day before; they won't get soggy!

—Amy Van Hemert, Ottumwa, IA

- -

Takes: 15 min. • **Makes:** 8 servings

- 1   carton (8 oz.) spreadable garden vegetable cream cheese
- 8   flour tortillas (8 in.)
- 4   cups fresh baby spinach
- 1   lb. sliced deli turkey

Spread cream cheese over tortillas. Layer with spinach and turkey. Roll up tightly; if not serving immediately, cover and refrigerate. To serve, cut the rolls crosswise into 1-in. slices.
6 pinwheels: 307 cal., 13g fat (6g sat. fat), 52mg chol., 866mg sod., 31g carb. (1g sugars, 2g fiber), 17g pro.

★ ★ ★ ★ ★ **READER REVIEW**

"I make these often with a few differences. I like to use plain cream cheese and add chopped dried cranberries. They're a big hit with everyone."

—LYNNWRIGHT, TASTEOFHOME.COM

STICKY HONEY
CHICKEN WINGS

ROASTED BUFFALO CAULIFLOWER BITES

ROASTED BUFFALO CAULIFLOWER BITES

Try these savory bites for a kickin' appetizer that's tasty and healthy, too!

—Emily Tyra, Lake Ann, MI

- -

Takes: 25 min. • **Makes:** 8 servings

- 1 **medium head cauliflower (about 2¼ lbs.), cut into florets**
- 1 **Tbsp. canola oil**
- ½ **cup Buffalo wing sauce**
  Blue cheese salad dressing

1. Preheat oven to 400°. Toss cauliflower with oil; spread in a 15x10x1-in. pan. Roast until tender and lightly browned, 20-25 minutes, stirring once.

2. Transfer to a bowl; toss with wing sauce. Serve with dressing.

⅓ cup: 39 cal., 2g fat (0 sat. fat), 0 chol., 474mg sod., 5g carb. (2g sugars, 2g fiber), 2g pro.

SPECIAL STUFFED STRAWBERRIES

These sweet bites can be made ahead of time, and they look really colorful on a tray. I will sometimes sprinkle the piped filling with finely chopped pistachio nuts.

—Marcia Orlando, Boyertown, PA

- -

Takes: 20 min. • **Makes:** 2 dozen

- 24 **large fresh strawberries**
- ½ **cup spreadable strawberry cream cheese**
- 3 **Tbsp. sour cream**
  Graham cracker crumbs

1. Place strawberries on a cutting board and cut off tops; remove bottom tips so they sit flat. Using a small paring knife, hull out the center of each berry.

2. In a small bowl, beat cream cheese and sour cream until smooth. Pipe or spoon filling into each berry. Top with crushed graham crackers. Refrigerate until serving.

1 strawberry: 18 cal., 1g fat (1g sat. fat), 4mg chol., 22mg sod., 1g carb. (1g sugars, 0 fiber), 1g pro.

NO-BAKE PEANUT BUTTER ENERGY BARS

This easy granola bar recipe is healthier than most. It's made with natural ingredients, and no baking is required! You can substitute sunflower seeds for the walnuts. Want more fiber? Add a little wheat germ.

—Amy Crane, Richland, MI

- -

Prep: 10 min. + chilling
Makes: 24 servings

- 1   cup creamy peanut butter
- 1   cup honey
- 4   cups quick-cooking oats
- 1   cup chopped walnuts
- ½   cup raisins
- ¼   tsp. salt

In a large microwave-safe bowl, combine peanut butter and honey. Heat, uncovered, until warmed, 20-30 seconds. Stir until smooth; add remaining ingredients and stir until combined. Transfer to a lightly greased 13x9-in. pan; gently press mixture into pan. Cover the pan and refrigerate until bars are set, 1 hour or overnight. Cut into squares.

1 bar: 197 cal., 10g fat (2g sat. fat), 0 chol., 71mg sod., 26g carb. (15g sugars, 2g fiber), 5g pro.

NO-BAKE PEANUT BUTTER ENERGY BARS

ROASTED CURRY CHICKPEAS

We coated chickpeas with simple seasonings to make this low-fat snacking sensation. It rivals the types sold in stores, with just a few ingredients.

—*Taste of Home* Test Kitchen

- -

Takes: 30 min. • **Makes:** 1 cup

- 1   can (15 oz.) chickpeas or garbanzo beans
- 2   Tbsp. olive oil
- 1   tsp. salt
- ¼   tsp. pepper
- 2   tsp. curry powder
- ½   tsp. crushed red pepper flakes

Preheat oven to 450°. Rinse and drain chickpeas. Place on paper towels; pat dry. Place in a greased 15x10x1-in. baking pan; drizzle with oil and sprinkle with seasonings. Toss to coat. Bake until crispy and golden brown, 25-30 minutes.

¼ cup: 162 cal., 9g fat (1g sat. fat), 0 chol., 728mg sod., 17g carb. (3g sugars, 5g fiber), 4g pro.

TEST KITCHEN TIP
Curry powder is a blend of many different ground spices used to replicate the individual spices combined in the cuisine of India. It imparts a distinctive flavor, a rich golden color to recipes and can be found in both mild and hot versions. Most cooks season dishes lightly with curry powder and add more as desired to reach an acceptable spice level.

**SLOW-COOKER
CHEESE DIP**

SLOW-COOKER CHEESE DIP

*I brought this slightly spicy dip
to a gathering with friends and
it was a huge hit. The spicy pork
sausage gives the dip plenty
of zip!*

—Marion Bartone, Conneaut, OH

Prep: 15 min. • **Cook:** 4 hours
Makes: 32 servings (2 qt.)

  1 lb. ground beef
  ½ lb. bulk spicy pork sausage
  2 lbs. cubed Velveeta
  2 cans (10 oz. each) diced
    tomatoes and green chiles
    Tortilla chip scoops, red
    pepper and cucumber sticks

1. In a large skillet, cook beef and
sausage over medium heat until
no longer pink; drain. Transfer to
a 3- or 4-qt. slow cooker. Stir in the
cheese and tomatoes.
2. Cover and cook on low for
4-5 hours or until cheese melts,
stirring occasionally. Serve with
tortilla chips, red pepper and
cucumber sticks.
¼ cup: 139 cal., 10g fat (5g sat. fat),
40mg chol., 486mg sod., 3g carb. (2g
sugars, 0 fiber), 8g pro

SUMMERTIME TEA

SUMMERTIME TEA

You can't have a sunny summer gathering around here without this sweet tea to cool you down. It's wonderful for sipping while basking in the sun by the pool.
—Angela Lively, Conroe, TX

- -

Prep: 15 min. + chilling
Makes: 18 servings

- 14 cups water, divided
- 6   black tea bags
- 1½ cups sugar
- ¾   cup thawed orange juice concentrate
- ¾   cup thawed lemonade concentrate
- 1   cup tequila, optional
   Optional: Fresh mint leaves and lemon or lime slices

1. In a large saucepan, bring 4 cups water to a boil. Remove from the heat; add tea bags. Cover and steep for 3-5 minutes. Discard tea bags.
2. Stir in the sugar, concentrates and remaining water. Add tequila if desired. Refrigerate until chilled. Garnish with mint and lemon if desired.
¾ cup: 102 cal., 0 fat (0 sat. fat), 0 chol., 1mg sod., 26g carb. (26g sugars, 0 fiber), 0 pro.

★ ★ ★ ★ ★ **READER REVIEW**
"So refreshing! I added 3 cups tequila to this variation on Texas tea to give it more of a kick. It was a hit at our dinner party."
—LESLEIGH5, TASTEOFHOME.COM

SIMMERED
SMOKED LINKS

SIMMERED SMOKED LINKS

No one can resist the sweet and spicy glaze on these bite-sized sausages. They're effortless to prepare, and they make a perfect party nibbler. Serve them on frilled toothpicks to make them extra fancy.

—Maxine Cenker, Weirton, WV

- -

Prep: 5 min. • **Cook:** 4 hours
Makes: about 6½ dozen

- 2 pkg. (16 oz. each) miniature smoked sausage links
- 1 cup packed brown sugar
- ½ cup ketchup
- ¼ cup prepared horseradish

Place sausages in a 3-qt. slow cooker. Combine the brown sugar, ketchup and horseradish; pour mixture over sausages. Cover and cook on low for 4 hours.

1 sausage: 46 cal., 3g fat (1g sat. fat), 7mg chol., 136mg sod., 3g carb. (3g sugars, 0 fiber), 1g pro.

TURKEY TEA SANDWICHES WITH BASIL MAYONNAISE

TURKEY TEA SANDWICHES WITH BASIL MAYONNAISE

Basil mayonnaise is the secret to these tasty little sandwiches. Keep extra mayo in the fridge to spread on other sandwiches, stir into egg salad or layer on pizza crust before topping it with other ingredients.

—Lara Pennell, Mauldin, SC

- -

Takes: 15 min.
Makes: 20 tea sandwiches

- ½ cup mayonnaise
- ⅓ cup loosely packed basil leaves
- 10 slices white bread, crusts removed
- 10 oz. thinly sliced deli turkey
- 5 slices provolone cheese

Place mayonnaise and basil in a food processor; process until basil is finely chopped, scraping down the sides as needed. Spread mayonnaise mixture over each bread slice. Layer 5 bread slices with turkey and cheese; top with remaining bread slices. Cut each into 4 long pieces.

1 tea sandwich: 90 cal., 6g fat (2g sat. fat), 9mg chol., 230mg sod., 4g carb. (0 sugars, 0 fiber), 5g pro.

ROASTED BRUSSELS SPROUTS WITH SRIRACHA AIOLI

This dish constantly surprises you—it's crispy, easy to eat, totally sharable and yet it's a vegetable! This recipe is also gluten-free, dairy-free and paleo-friendly, and can be vegan if you use vegan mayo.
—Molly Winsten, Medford, MA

- -

Prep: 20 min. • **Cook:** 20 min.
 Makes: 8 servings

- 1   lb. fresh Brussels sprouts, trimmed and halved
- 2   Tbsp. olive oil
- 2   to 4 tsp. Sriracha chili sauce, divided
- ½   tsp. salt, divided
- ½   tsp. pepper, divided
- ½   cup mayonnaise
- 2   tsp. lime juice
- 1   Tbsp. lemon juice

1. Preheat oven to 425°. Place Brussels sprouts on a rimmed baking sheet. Drizzle with oil and 1 tsp. chili sauce; sprinkle with ¼ tsp. salt and ¼ tsp. pepper. Toss to coat. Roast until crispy, 20-25 minutes.
2. Meanwhile, mix mayonnaise, lime juice, and the remaining 1-3 tsp. chili sauce, ¼ tsp. salt and ¼ tsp. pepper. Drizzle lemon juice over Brussels sprouts before serving with the aioli.
4 halves with 1 Tbsp. sauce: 146 cal., 14g fat (2g sat. fat), 1mg chol., 310mg sod., 6g carb. (2g sugars, 2g fiber), 2g pro.

CRAB CRESCENTS

These elegant little spiral-wrapped bites are delicious, decadent and easy to make— the perfect combination for a holiday party!
—Stephanie Howard, Oakland, CA

- -

Takes: 25 min. • **Makes:** 16 appetizers

- 1   tube (8 oz.) refrigerated crescent rolls
- 3   Tbsp. prepared pesto
- ½   cup fresh crabmeat

1. Preheat the oven to 375°. Unroll the crescent dough; separate into 8 triangles. Cut each triangle in half lengthwise, forming 2 triangles. Spread ½ tsp. pesto over each triangle; place 1 rounded tsp. of crab along the wide end of each triangle.
2. Roll up triangles from the wide ends and place point side down 1 in. apart on an ungreased baking sheet.
3. Bake 10-12 minutes, or until golden brown. Serve warm.
1 piece: 74 cal., 4g fat (1g sat. fat), 5mg chol., 144mg sod., 6g carb. (1g sugars, 0 fiber), 2g pro.

CRAB CRESCENTS

ROSY
APPLESAUCE

ROSY APPLESAUCE

*I end up with lots of rhubarb
each summer, but many of the
recipes use a lot of sugar. This
one relies mostly on the fruit to
sweeten up the rhubarb instead.
I refrigerate the sauce overnight
to help the flavors blend.*
—Amy Nelson, Weston, WI

- -

Prep: 25 min. • **Cook:** 25 min.
Makes: 6 cups

- 5 **large Red Delicious apples,
  peeled and finely chopped**
- 4 **cups finely chopped fresh
  or thawed frozen rhubarb
  (about 8 stalks)**

- 4 **cups fresh strawberries,
  hulled and halved**
- ½ **cup sugar**
- ¼ **cup water**
- 1 **tsp. vanilla extract**

1. In a Dutch oven, combine the
apples, rhubarb, strawberries, sugar
and water; bring mixture to a boil.
Reduce the heat; simmer, covered,
18-22 minutes or until fruit is tender,
stirring occasionally.
2. Remove from heat; stir in vanilla.
If a smoother consistency is desired,
cool slightly and, in batches, process
in a blender. Serve warm or cold.
Freeze option: Freeze cooled
applesauce in freezer containers.
To use, thaw in refrigerator overnight.

Serve cold or heat through in a
saucepan, stirring occasionally.
½ cup: 93 cal., 0 fat (0 sat. fat),
0 chol., 2mg sod., 23g carb. (19g
sugars, 3g fiber), 1g pro. **Diabetic
exchanges:** 1 fruit, ½ starch.

TEST KITCHEN TIP
This fruity applesauce
makes a delightful healthy
snack, but don't stop there.
Consider serving a small
portion of it alongside
smoked pork chops or
barbecued chicken.

**APPLE-GOUDA
PIGS IN A BLANKET**

APPLE-GOUDA
PIGS IN A BLANKET

*For New Year's, I used to make
pigs in a blanket with beef and
cheddar. But now I like apple
and Gouda for an even better
flavor celebration.*

—Megan Weiss, Menomonie, WI

- -

Takes: 30 min. • **Makes:** 2 dozen

- 1   **tube (8 oz.) refrigerated
      crescent rolls**
- 1   **small apple, peeled and cut
      into 24 thin slices**
- 6   **thin slices Gouda cheese,
      quartered**
- 24 **miniature smoked sausages
      Honey mustard salad
      dressing, optional**

1. Preheat oven to 375°. Unroll the
dough and separate into 8 triangles;
cut each lengthwise into 3 narrow
triangles. On the wide end of each,
place 1 apple slice, 1 folded piece of
cheese and 1 sausage; roll up tightly.

2. Place 1 in. apart on parchment-
lined baking sheets, point side
down. Bake until golden brown,
10-12 minutes. If desired, serve
with dressing.

1 appetizer: 82 cal., 6g fat (2g sat.
fat), 11mg chol., 203mg sod., 5g carb.
(1g sugars, 0 fiber), 3g pro.

SPARKLING COCONUT GRAPE JUICE

This sparkling drink is a nice change of pace from lemonade and party punch. The mix of lime, coconut and grape is so refreshing. Add a splash of gin if you're feeling bold.

—Shelly Bevington, Hermiston, OR

- -

Takes: 5 min. • **Makes:** 6 servings

- 4 **cups white grape juice**
- 2 **tsp. lime juice**
  Ice cubes
- 2 **cups coconut-flavored sparkling water, chilled**
  Optional: Lime wedges or slices

In a pitcher, combine grape juice and lime juice. Fill 6 tall glasses with ice. Pour the juice mixture evenly into glasses; top off with sparkling water. Stir to combine. Garnish with lime wedges if desired.

1 cup: 94 cal., 0 fat (0 sat. fat), 0 chol., 13mg sod., 24g carb. (21g sugars, 0 fiber), 0 pro.

SPARKLING COCONUT GRAPE JUICE

DREAMY FRUIT DIP

APPETIZER SHRIMP KABOBS

Talk about fuss-free! These skewers are simple to assemble, and they grill to perfection in minutes. My guests enjoy them with a spicy seafood sauce.
—Dianna Knight, Clayton, NC

- -

Prep: 10 min. + standing
Grill: 5 min. • **Makes:** 8 servings

  3 Tbsp. olive oil
  3 garlic cloves, crushed
  ½ cup dry bread crumbs
  ½ tsp. seafood seasoning
 32 uncooked medium shrimp (about 1 lb.), peeled and deveined
     Seafood cocktail sauce

1. In a shallow bowl, combine the oil and garlic; let stand for 30 minutes. In another bowl, combine bread crumbs and seafood seasoning. Dip shrimp in oil mixture, then coat with crumb mixture.

2. Thread onto metal or soaked wooden skewers. Grill kabobs, covered, over medium heat for 2-3 minutes or until shrimp turn pink. Serve with seafood sauce.

1 serving: 133 cal., 6g fat (1g sat. fat), 86mg chol., 142mg sod., 6g carb. (0 sugars, 1g fiber), 12g pro.
Diabetic exchanges: 1½ lean meat, ½ starch.

DREAMY FRUIT DIP

Everyone will love this thick cream cheese fruit dip. Serve it with apple wedges, pineapple chunks, strawberries and grapes.
—Anna Beiler, Strasburg, PA

- -

Takes: 10 min. • **Makes:** about 4 cups

  1 pkg. (8 oz.) cream cheese, softened
  ½ cup butter, softened
  ½ cup marshmallow creme
  1 carton (8 oz.) frozen whipped topping, thawed
     Assorted fresh fruit

In a small bowl, beat cream cheese and butter until smooth. Beat in marshmallow creme. Fold in the whipped topping. Serve with fruit. Store in the refrigerator.

2 Tbsp.: 75 cal., 6g fat (5g sat. fat), 15mg chol., 51mg sod., 3g carb. (2g sugars, 0 fiber), 1g pro.

TEST KITCHEN TIP
You can chill leftover dip for a tasty topping for toast the next morning.

APPETIZER
SHRIMP KABOBS

EASY PIMIENTO
CHEESE

EASY PIMIENTO CHEESE

Every good Southerner has their own version of pimiento cheese. It's wonderful on crackers, in a sandwich with fresh summer tomatoes or inside a grilled cheese sandwich

—Josh Carter, Birmingham, AL

- -

Prep: 15 min. + chilling
Makes: 16 servings

- 1⅓ cups mayonnaise
- 2 jars (4 oz. each) pimiento strips, chopped
- 1½ tsp. Worcestershire sauce
- ¼ tsp. cayenne pepper
- ¼ tsp. pepper
- 1 block (8 oz.) sharp cheddar cheese, shredded
- 1 block (8 oz.) extra-sharp cheddar cheese, shredded

In a large bowl, combine the first 5 ingredients. Add cheeses and stir to combine. Refrigerate, covered, at least 1 hour.

¼ cup: 238 cal., 23g fat (7g sat. fat), 29mg chol., 286mg sod., 2g carb. (1g sugars, 0 fiber), 7g pro.`

GINGER-ORANGE REFRESHER

With or without the rum, my two-tone drink will impress party guests. You can use another citrus fruit in place of the oranges if you'd like.

—Marybeth Mank, Mesquite, TX

- -

Prep: 15 min.
Cook: 15 min. + cooling
Makes: 10 servings

- 3 medium oranges
- 1½ cups turbinado (washed raw) sugar
- 1½ cups water
- 1 cup fresh mint leaves
- 8 slices fresh gingerroot
  Crushed ice
- 5 oz. spiced rum, optional
- 1 bottle (1 liter) club soda, chilled

1. Using a vegetable peeler, remove colored layer of peel from oranges in strips, leaving the white pith. Cut oranges crosswise in half; squeeze juice from oranges.

2. In a small saucepan, combine sugar, water and orange juice; bring to a boil. Stir in mint, ginger and orange peel; return to a boil. Reduce heat; simmer, uncovered, for 10 minutes. Cool the syrup mixture completely.

3. Strain syrup, discarding solids. To serve, fill 10 highball glasses halfway with ice. Add 2 oz. syrup and, if desired, ½ oz. rum to each glass; top with soda.

1 serving: 134 cal., 0 fat (0 sat. fat), 0 chol., 25mg sod., 34g carb. (32g sugars, 1g fiber), 1g pro.

PIZZA OYSTER CRACKERS

This quick and easy snack is a favorite of my kids. I always include a baggie in their lunchboxes.

—Carol S. Betz, Grand Rapids, MI

- -

Takes: 10 min.
Makes: 12 cups (24 servings)

- 2 pkg. (9 oz. each) oyster crackers
- ½ cup canola oil
- ⅓ cup grated Parmesan cheese
- ¼ cup pizza seasoning or Italian seasoning
- ½ tsp. garlic powder

1. Preheat oven to 350°. Place the crackers in a large bowl. In a small bowl, mix the oil, cheese, pizza seasoning and garlic powder; pour over crackers and toss gently to coat. Transfer crackers to 2 ungreased 15x10x1-in. baking pans.

2. Bake 5-7 minutes, stirring once. Cool. Store in an airtight container.

½ cup: 135 cal., 7g fat (1g sat. fat), 1mg chol., 220mg sod., 16g carb. (0 sugars, 1g fiber), 2g pro.

GINGER-ORANGE REFRESHER

EASY CHEESE-STUFFED JALAPENOS

EASY CHEESE-STUFFED JALAPENOS

A few years ago, I saw a man in the grocery store buying a big bag of jalapeno peppers. I asked him what he intended to do with them, and right there in the store he gave me this fabulous recipe for stuffed jalapenos!

—Janice Montiverdi, Sugar Land, TX

Prep: 30 min. • **Bake:** 5 min.
Makes: 4 dozen

24   medium fresh jalapeno peppers
1   pkg. (8 oz.) cream cheese, softened
3   cups finely shredded cheddar cheese
1½   tsp. Worcestershire sauce
4   bacon strips, cooked and crumbled

1. Preheat oven to 400°. Cut jalapenos in half lengthwise; remove seeds and membranes. In a large saucepan, boil peppers in water for 5-10 minutes (the longer you boil the peppers, the milder they will be). Drain and rinse in cold water; set aside.

2. In a small bowl, beat the cream cheese, cheddar cheese and Worcestershire sauce until smooth. Spoon 2 teaspoons mixture into each jalapeno; sprinkle with bacon. Arrange on greased baking sheets. Bake 3-5 minutes, or until filling is warmed.

Note: Wear disposable gloves when cutting hot peppers; the oils can burn skin. Avoid touching your face.

1 piece: 141 cal., 12g fat (8g sat. fat), 39mg chol., 200mg sod., 3g carb. (0 sugars, 1g fiber), 6g pro.

CANDIED WALNUTS

CANDIED WALNUTS

Turn ordinary walnuts into a taste sensation with this simple recipe that's prepared on the stovetop. With plenty of brown sugar and a hint of pepper, the crunchy candied nuts are a nice complement to a cheese and fruit tray. But they can stand on their own as well, because they're so munchable!

—*Taste of Home* Test Kitchen

- - - - - - - - - - - - - - - - - - - -

Takes: 20 min. • **Makes:** 2 cups

- 2 **Tbsp. canola oil**
- 2 **Tbsp. balsamic vinegar**

⅛ **tsp. pepper**
2 **cups walnut halves**
½ **cup packed brown sugar**

1. In a large heavy skillet, combine the oil, vinegar and pepper. Cook and stir over medium heat until blended. Add walnuts and cook over medium heat until nuts are toasted, about 4 minutes.

2. Sprinkle with brown sugar. Cook and stir until the sugar is melted, 2-4 minutes. Spread on foil to cool. Store in an airtight container.

2 Tbsp.: 124 cal., 10g fat (1g sat. fat), 0 chol., 3mg sod., 9g carb. (7g sugars, 1g fiber), 2g pro.

★ ★ ★ ★ ★ **READER REVIEW**
"It's delicious. The first batch went so quickly that I have to make some more. Great for salads!"
—DTDAVIES, TASTEOFHOME.COM

**PEPPER JELLY HOGS
IN A BLANKET**

PEPPER JELLY HOGS IN A BLANKET

We are addicted to these grown-up pigs in a blanket! There's so much flavor for such bite-sized appetizers.
—Becky Hardin, St. Peters, MO

- -

Prep: 20 min. • **Bake:** 15 min.
Makes: 2 dozen

- 1 tube (8 oz.) refrigerated crescent rolls
- 1 pkg. (12 oz.) fully cooked spicy sausage links, cut into 1-in. slices
- ¼ cup pepper jelly
  Stone-ground mustard

1. Preheat oven to 375°. Coat 24 mini muffin cups with cooking spray.
2. Unroll crescent dough and separate into 2 rectangles; press perforations to seal. Cut dough lengthwise into ¾-in. strips. Wrap a strip of dough around a sausage slice, gently stretching dough as you roll. Place cut side up in a muffin cup; repeat with remaining dough and sausage. Spoon pepper jelly over each slice.
3. Bake the hogs until golden brown, 12-15 minutes. Let stand 5 minutes before removing to a serving plate. Serve warm with mustard.
1 appetizer: 65 cal., 3g fat (0 sat. fat), 11mg chol., 152mg sod., 7g carb. (3g sugars, 0 fiber), 3g pro.

CHILI & JELLY MEATBALLS

CHILI & JELLY MEATBALLS

The secret ingredient in this sassy sauce is the grape jelly. It's a sweet contrast with the chili sauce.
—Irma Schnuelle, Manitowoc, WI

- -

Takes: 30 min.
Makes: about 3 dozen

- 2 pkg. (22 oz. each) frozen fully cooked Angus beef meatballs
- 1 bottle (12 oz.) chili sauce
- 1 jar (10 oz.) grape jelly

1. Prepare meatballs according to the package instructions.
2. In a large skillet, combine chili sauce and jelly; cook and stir over medium heat until jelly has melted. Add meatballs to pan; heat through.
1 meatball: 106 cal., 6g fat (3g sat. fat), 17mg chol., 313mg sod., 8g carb. (6g sugars, 0 fiber), 4g pro.

GARLIC-HERB MINI QUICHES

Looking for a wonderful little bite to dress up your brunch buffet? These delectable tartlets are irresistible!
—Josephine Piro, Easton, PA

- -

Takes: 25 min.
Makes: 45 mini quiches

1 **pkg. (6½ oz.) reduced-fat garlic-herb spreadable cheese**
¼ **cup fat-free milk**
2 **large eggs**
3 **pkg. (1.9 oz. each) frozen miniature phyllo tart shells**
2 **Tbsp. minced fresh parsley**
  Minced chives, optional

1. Preheat oven to 350°. In a small bowl, beat spreadable cheese, milk and eggs. Place the tart shells on an ungreased baking sheet; fill each with 2 tsp. mixture. Sprinkle with parsley.
2. Bake for 10-12 minutes or until filling is set and shells are lightly browned. Sprinkle with chives if desired. Serve warm.
1 mini quiche: 31 cal., 2g fat (0 sat. fat), 12mg chol., 32mg sod., 2g carb. (0 sugars, 0 fiber), 1g pro.

BACON-WRAPPED SHRIMP

I tweaked this recipe to please my family, and now it's a hit! For less heat, skip the jalapenos.
—Debbie Cheek, State Road, NC

- -

Prep: 25 min. + marinating
Broil: 5 min. • **Makes:** 2½ dozen

30 **uncooked shrimp (31-40 per lb.), peeled and deveined**
6 **Tbsp. creamy Caesar salad dressing, divided**
15 **bacon strips, halved crosswise**
2 **jalapeno peppers, seeded and thinly sliced**

1. Preheat broiler. In a large bowl, toss shrimp with 4 Tbsp. dressing; let stand 15 minutes.
2. Meanwhile, in a large skillet, cook bacon over medium heat until partially cooked but not crisp. Remove to paper towels to drain; keep warm.
3. Drain shrimp, discarding the marinade. Top each shrimp with a jalapeno slice and wrap with a bacon strip; secure with a toothpick. Place on a greased rack of a broiler pan.
4. Broil 4 in. from heat 2-3 minutes on each side or until the shrimp turn pink, basting them frequently with remaining dressing after turning.
Note: Wear disposable gloves when cutting hot peppers; the oils can burn skin. Avoid touching your face.
1 appetizer: 34 cal., 2g fat (1g sat. fat), 26mg chol., 113mg sod., 0 carb. (0 sugars, 0 fiber), 4g pro. **Diabetic exchanges:** 1 lean meat.

BACON-WRAPPED SHRIMP

MARINARA-MOZZARELLA DIP

MARINARA-MOZZARELLA DIP

Talk about easy! With three ingredients and two loaves of baguette-style French bread, you have an easy appetizer that will please your family and guests. For variety, try using goat cheese instead of mozzarella cheese.

—Janie Colle, Hutchinson, KS

- -

Prep: 10 min. • **Cook:** 2½ hours
Makes: 12 servings (3 cups)

2 cups marinara sauce
1 carton (8 oz.) fresh mozzarella cheese pearls, drained
2 Tbsp. minced fresh basil
French bread baguette, thinly sliced and toasted
Optional: Crushed red pepper flakes and additional fresh minced basil

Pour marinara into a 1½-qt. slow cooker. Cook, covered, on low until hot, about 2 hours. Stir in mozzarella and basil. Cook until the cheese is melted, about 30 minutes longer. If desired, top with crushed red pepper flakes and additional basil. Serve with toasted baguette slices.

¼ **cup:** 76 cal., 5g fat (3g sat. fat), 16mg chol., 219mg sod., 4g carb. (3g sugars, 1g fiber), 4g pro.

TEST KITCHEN TIP
This recipe works well with jarred pasta sauce, so use your favorite brand and flavor.

SAVORY
CUCUMBER
SANDWICHES

SAVORY CUCUMBER SANDWICHES

Italian salad dressing is an easy way to add zip to this simple spread. You can also use it as a dip with crackers and veggies or a sandwich filling.

—Carol Henderson, Chagrin Falls, OH

- -

Prep: 15 min. + chilling
Makes: 3 dozen

- 1 **pkg. (8 oz.) cream cheese, softened**
- ½ **cup mayonnaise**
- 1 **envelope Italian salad dressing mix**
- 36 **slices snack rye bread**
- 1 **medium cucumber, sliced**
  Snipped fresh dill, optional

1. In a small bowl, combine the cream cheese, mayonnaise and salad dressing mix. Refrigerate for 1 hour.
2. Just before serving, spread over each slice of rye bread; top each with a cucumber slice. If desired, sprinkle with dill.

1 sandwich: 62 cal., 5g fat (2g sat. fat), 7mg chol., 149mg sod., 4g carb. (1g sugars, 0 fiber), 1g pro.

FAVORITE HOT CHOCOLATE

You need just a few basic ingredients to stir up this spirit-warming sipper. The comforting beverage is smooth and not too sweet, making it just right for a cozy, chilly night.

—Flo Snodderly, North Vernon, IN

- -

Takes: 15 min. • **Makes:** 8 servings

- 1 **can (14 oz.) sweetened condensed milk**
- ½ **cup baking cocoa**
- 6½ **cups water**
- 2 **tsp. vanilla extract**
  Optional: Sweetened whipped cream, marshmallows, chocolate syrup and Pirouette cookies

1. Place milk and cocoa in a large saucepan; cook and stir over medium heat until blended. Gradually stir in water; heat through, stirring occasionally.
2. Remove from heat; stir in vanilla. Add toppings as desired.

1 cup: 177 cal., 5g fat (3g sat. fat), 17mg chol., 63mg sod., 30g carb. (27g sugars, 1g fiber), 5g pro.

★ ★ ★ ★ ★ **READER REVIEW**

"The phone was ringing all day long: 'I need that recipe; I loved it!' Served at a school party for Christmas."

—KACATJ, TASTEOFHOME.COM

**FAVORITE
HOT CHOCOLATE**

GREEK OLIVE TAPENADE

PRINCESS TOAST

I made these sparkly treats for my daughter's Brownie troop and they're great for princess parties. Sometimes I use lemon curd in place of the jam.
—Marina Castle Kelley,
Canyon Country, CA

- -

Takes: 10 min. • **Makes:** 6 servings

6	slices white bread, toasted
6	Tbsp. seedless strawberry jam
1½	cups buttercream frosting
6	Tbsp. sprinkles
6	tsp. silver or gold edible glitter

Spread jam over toast. Top with buttercream, sprinkles and edible glitter. Leave toasts whole or cut into shapes.
Note: Edible glitter is available from Wilton Industries. Call 800-794-5866 or visit wilton.com.
1 piece: 465 cal., 13g fat (5g sat. fat), 0 chol., 284mg sod., 82g carb. (58g sugars, 1g fiber), 3g pro.

TEST KITCHEN TIP
Here's a fun way for kids to get creative in the kitchen. Mix up the frosting colors and toppings to match the season and your children's preferences. Fresh fruit and cream cheese make great toppers, too.

GREEK OLIVE TAPENADE

Welcome to an olive lover's dream. Mix olives with freshly minced garlic, parsley and a few drizzles of olive oil to have the ultimate in Mediterranean bliss.
—Lisa Sojka, Rockport, ME

- -

Takes: 25 min.
Makes: 16 servings (about 2 cups)

2	cups pitted Greek olives, drained
3	garlic cloves, minced
3	Tbsp. olive oil
1½	tsp. minced fresh parsley
	Toasted baguette slices

In a food processor, pulse olives with garlic until finely chopped. Add oil and parsley; pulse until combined. Serve with toasted baguette slices.
2 Tbsp. tapenade: 71 cal., 7g fat (1g sat. fat), 0 chol., 277mg sod., 2g carb. (0 sugars, 0 fiber), 0 pro.

PRINCESS
TOAST

HONEY
HORSERADISH DIP

HONEY HORSERADISH DIP

We love having appetizers on Friday night instead of a meal, and during the summer we enjoy cooler foods. This has just the right amount of zing.

—Ann Marie Eberhart, Gig Harbor, WA

- -

Prep: 10 min. + chilling
Makes: 1 cup

- ½ cup fat-free plain Greek yogurt
- ¼ cup stone-ground mustard
- ¼ cup honey
- 2 Tbsp. prepared horseradish
  Cold cooked shrimp and fresh sugar snap peas

Combine yogurt, mustard, honey and horseradish; refrigerate 1 hour. Serve with shrimp and snap peas.

2 Tbsp.: 54 cal., 1g fat (0 sat. fat), 0 chol., 177mg sod., 11g carb. (10g sugars, 0 fiber), 2g pro. **Diabetic exchanges:** 1 starch.

BRIE WITH ALMONDS

This nut-topped cheese is elegant and impressive for holiday occasions. No one will guess that the recipe is actually a snap to prepare.

—Mildred Aydt, Chanhassen, MN

- -

Takes: 15 min. • **Makes:** 8 servings

- 1 round Brie cheese (8 oz.)
- 2 Tbsp. butter, melted
- ¼ cup sliced almonds
- 1 Tbsp. brandy, optional
  Assorted crackers or fresh vegetables

1. Preheat oven to 400°. Place Brie in a small ungreased cast-iron skillet or shallow 1-qt. baking dish. Combine the butter, almonds and, if desired, brandy; pour over Brie.
2. Bake, uncovered, until cheese is softened, 10-12 minutes. Serve with crackers or vegetables.

1 serving: 141 cal., 12g fat (7g sat. fat), 36mg chol., 199mg sod., 1g carb. (0 sugars, 0 fiber), 7g pro.

CRABBIE PHYLLO CUPS

I always like a dot of extra chili sauce on top of these easy snacks. If you're out of crab, water-packed tuna works well, too.

—Johnna Johnson, Scottsdale, AZ

Takes: 20 min. • **Makes:** 2½ dozen

½ cup reduced-fat spreadable garden vegetable cream cheese

½ tsp. seafood seasoning
¾ cup lump crabmeat, drained
2 pkg. (1.9 oz. each) frozen miniature phyllo tart shells
5 Tbsp. chili sauce

In a small bowl, mix cream cheese and seafood seasoning; gently stir in crab. Spoon 2 tsp. crab mixture into each tart shell; top with chili sauce.

1 filled phyllo cup: 34 cal., 2g fat (0 sat. fat), 5mg chol., 103mg sod., 3g carb. (1g sugars, 0 fiber), 1g pro.

CRABBIE PHYLLO CUPS

CREAMY WASABI SPREAD

Sesame seeds can create an attractive coating on this easy cracker spread. Be sure to watch when you're toasting the seeds; they burn easily. You can use any flavor of rice cracker, but the wasabi variety is great.

—Tammie Balon, Boyce, VA

Takes: 10 min. • **Makes:** 8 servings

1 pkg. (8 oz.) cream cheese
¼ cup prepared wasabi
2 Tbsp. sesame seeds, toasted
2 Tbsp. soy sauce
Rice crackers

1. Place cream cheese on a cutting board; split into 2 layers. Spread the wasabi over the bottom half; replace top layer.
2. Press both sides of block into sesame seeds. Place on a shallow serving plate; pour soy sauce around the cheese. Serve with crackers.

1 oz.: 135 cal., 11g fat (6g sat. fat), 31mg chol., 483mg sod., 6g carb. (0 sugars, 0 fiber), 3g pro.

TEST KITCHEN TIP
Wasabi, a Japanese horseradish, is bright green in color and has a sharp, pungent and fiery-hot flavor. It is traditionally used as a condiment with sushi and sashimi. Today, many western sauces, mustards and other condiments are seasoned with wasabi. Wasabi powder and paste are also available in the Asian food section.

PROSCIUTTO-WRAPPED ASPARAGUS WITH RASPBERRY SAUCE

PROSCIUTTO-WRAPPED ASPARAGUS WITH RASPBERRY SAUCE

Grilling the prosciutto with the asparagus gives this appetizer a salty crunch that's perfect for dipping into a sweet glaze. When a delicious appetizer is this easy to prepare, you owe it to yourself to try it!
—Noelle Myers, Grand Forks, ND

- -

Takes: 30 min. • **Makes:** 16 appetizers

⅓ lb. thinly sliced prosciutto or deli ham
16 fresh asparagus spears, trimmed
½ cup seedless raspberry jam
2 Tbsp. balsamic vinegar

1. Cut prosciutto slices in half. Wrap a prosciutto piece around each asparagus spear; secure ends with toothpicks.
2. Grill asparagus, covered, on an oiled rack over medium heat for 6-8 minutes or until the prosciutto is crisp, turning once. Discard toothpicks.
3. In a small microwave-safe bowl, microwave jam and vinegar on high for 15-20 seconds or until jam is melted. Serve with asparagus.
1 asparagus spear with 1½ tsp. sauce: 50 cal., 1g fat (0 sat. fat), 8mg chol., 184mg sod., 7g carb. (7g sugars, 0 fiber), 3g pro. **Diabetic exchanges:** ½ starch.

PRESSURE-COOKER
HOMEMADE CHUNKY
APPLESAUCE

PRESSURE-COOKER HOMEMADE CHUNKY APPLESAUCE

This applesauce is so easy. My family loves the things I make from scratch, and it's good knowing exactly what I'm putting in it!
—Marilee Cardinal, Burlington, NJ

- -

Prep: 10 min.
Cook: 5 min. + releasing
Makes: 5 cups

7   medium McIntosh, Empire or other apples (about 3 lbs.)
½   cup sugar
½   cup water
1   Tbsp. lemon juice
¼   tsp. almond or vanilla extract

1. Peel, core and cut each apple into 8 wedges. Cut each wedge crosswise in half; place apples in a 6-qt. electric pressure cooker. Add remaining ingredients.
2. Lock lid; close pressure-release valve. Adjust to pressure-cook on high for 3 minutes. Let pressure release naturally. Mash apples with a potato masher or use an immersion blender until sauce is desired consistency.

¾ cup: 139 cal., 0 fat (0 sat. fat), 0 chol., 0 sod., 36g carb. (33g sugars, 2g fiber), 0 pro.

SKILLET MAC & CHEESE
P. 84

BREADS, SALADS & SIDE DISHES

1

2

3

4

5

ROUND OUT YOUR MEAL WITH ONE OF THE DELICIOUS, SAVORY DISHES IN THIS GO-TO CHAPTER.

MINTY PEAS & ONIONS

MINTY PEAS & ONIONS

Mother always relied on peas and onions when she was in a hurry and needed a quick side dish. Simple to prepare, this dish was loved by everyone. It was handed down to my mother by my grandmother.

—Santa D'Addario, Jacksonville, FL

- -

Takes: 20 min. • **Makes:** 8 servings

- 2 **large onions,** **cut into ½-in. wedges**
- ½ **cup chopped sweet** **red pepper**
- 2 **Tbsp. vegetable oil**
- 2 **pkg. (16 oz. each) frozen peas**
- 2 **Tbsp. minced fresh mint or** **2 tsp. dried mint**

In a large skillet, saute onions and red pepper in oil until onions just begin to soften. Add the peas; cook, uncovered, stirring occasionally, for 10 minutes or until heated through. Stir in mint and cook for 1 minute.

1 serving: 134 cal., 4g fat (1g sat. fat), 0 chol., 128mg sod., 19g carb. (9g sugars, 6g fiber), 6g pro.
Diabetic exchanges: 1 starch, 1 fat.

MILK-AND-HONEY WHITE BREAD

Honey adds special flavor to this traditional white bread.

—Kathy McCreary, Goddard, KS

- -

Prep: 15 min. + rising
Bake: 30 min. + cooling
Makes: 2 loaves (16 pieces each)

MILK-AND-HONEY WHITE BREAD

- 2 **pkg. (¼ oz. each) active** **dry yeast**
- 2½ **cups warm 2% milk** **(110° to 115°)**
- ⅓ **cup honey**
- ¼ **cup butter, melted**
- 2 **tsp. salt**
- 8 **to 8½ cups all-purpose flour**

1. In a large bowl, dissolve yeast in warm milk. Add honey, butter, salt and 5 cups flour; beat until smooth. Add enough remaining flour to form a soft dough.

2. Turn onto a floured board; knead the dough until smooth and elastic, 6-8 minutes. Place in a greased bowl, turning once to grease top. Cover and let dough rise in a warm place until doubled, about 1 hour.

3. Preheat oven to 375°. Punch the dough down and shape into 2 loaves. Place each in a greased 9x5-in. loaf pan. Cover pans and let dough rise until doubled, about 30 minutes.

4. Bake 30-35 minutes or until golden brown. Cover loosely with foil if top browns too quickly. Remove from pans and cool on wire racks.

1 piece: 149 cal., 2g fat (1g sat. fat), 6mg chol., 172mg sod., 28g carb. (4g sugars, 1g fiber), 4g pro.

**AMBROSIA
SALAD**

AMBROSIA SALAD

*Because it's so simple to make,
this tropical medley is great as a
last-minute menu addition. Plus,
it requires just five ingredients.*
—Judi Bringegar, Liberty, NC

- -

Prep: 10 min. + chilling
Makes: 4 servings

- 1   can (15 oz.) mandarin
      oranges, drained
- 1   can (8 oz.) pineapple tidbits,
      drained
- 1   cup miniature marshmallows
- 1   cup sweetened shredded
      coconut
- 1   cup sour cream

In a large bowl, combine oranges,
pineapple, marshmallows and
coconut. Add the sour cream and
toss to mix. Cover and refrigerate
for several hours.

1 cup: 370 cal., 20g fat (14g sat. fat),
14mg chol., 101mg sod., 48g carb.
(43g sugars, 2g fiber), 4g pro.

★ ★ ★ ★ ★ **READER REVIEW**
"A holiday staple since
I was a kid! We call it
5-cup salad for the
5 ingredients. I have
to make a double
recipe so my mom
and husband have
leftovers! Delicious."

—SHARONHUGHART, TASTEOFHOME.COM

PERFECT DINNER ROLLS

These rolls melt in your mouth. I loved them as a child, and I'm happy to now make them for my kids because I know I am creating those same delicious memories my mom made for me!

—Gayleen Grote, Battleview, ND

- -

Prep: 30 min. + rising • **Bake:** 15 min.
Makes: 2 dozen

- 1 Tbsp. active dry yeast
- 2¼ cups warm water (110° to 115°)
- ⅓ cup sugar
- ⅓ cup shortening
- ¼ cup powdered nondairy creamer
- 2¼ tsp. salt
- 6 to 7 cups bread flour

1. In a large bowl, dissolve the yeast in warm water. Add sugar, shortening, creamer, salt and 5 cups flour. Beat dough until smooth. Stir in enough of the remaining flour to form a soft dough (it will be sticky).

2. Turn onto a floured surface; knead the dough until smooth and elastic, 6-8 minutes. Place in a bowl coated with cooking spray, turning once to coat top. Cover and let rise in a warm place until doubled, about 1 hour.

3. Punch dough down. Turn onto a lightly floured surface; divide into 24 pieces. Shape each into a roll. Place 2 in. apart on baking sheets coated with cooking spray. Cover and let rise until doubled, about 30 minutes.

4. Meanwhile, preheat the oven to 350°. Bake rolls until lightly browned, 12-15 minutes. Remove from pans to wire racks.

1 roll: 142 cal., 3g fat (1g sat. fat), 0 chol., 222mg sod., 25g carb. (3g sugars, 1g fiber), 4g pro.

HOMEMADE TORTILLAS

I usually have to double this recipe because we go through these tortillas so quickly. They are tender, chewy and so simple, you'll never use store-bought tortillas again.

—Kristin Van Dyken, Kennewick, WA

- -

Takes: 30 min. • **Makes:** 8 tortillas

- 2 cups all-purpose flour
- ½ tsp. salt
- ¾ cup water
- 3 Tbsp. olive oil

1. In a large bowl, combine flour and salt. Stir in water and oil. Turn onto a floured surface; knead 10-12 times; add a little flour or water if needed to achieve a smooth dough. Let rest for 10 minutes.

2. Divide dough into 8 portions. On a lightly floured surface, roll each portion into a 7-in. circle.

3. In a greased cast-iron or other heavy skillet, cook tortillas over medium heat until they are lightly browned, about 1 minute on each side. Serve warm.

1 tortilla: 159 cal., 5g fat (1g sat. fat), 0 chol., 148mg sod., 24g carb. (1g sugars, 1g fiber), 3g pro. **Diabetic exchanges:** 1½ starch, 1 fat.

PERFECT DINNER ROLLS

SIMPLE
BISCUITS

SIMPLE BISCUITS

It's easy to whip up a batch of these buttery biscuits to serve with breakfast or dinner. The dough is very easy to work with, so there's no need to roll with a rolling pin; just pat to the right thickness.
—*Taste of Home* Test Kitchen

Takes: 25 min. • **Makes:** 15 biscuits

- 2 **cups all-purpose flour**
- 3 **tsp. baking powder**
- 1 **tsp. salt**
- ⅓ **cup cold butter, cubed**
- ⅔ **cup 2% milk**

1. Preheat oven to 450°. In a large bowl, whisk flour, baking powder and salt. Cut in the butter until mixture resembles coarse crumbs. Add milk; stir just until moistened.

2. Turn onto a lightly floured surface; knead gently 8-10 times. Pat dough to ½-in. thickness. Cut rounds with a 2½-in. biscuit cutter.

3. Place 1 in. apart on an ungreased baking sheet. Bake until golden brown, 10-15 minutes. Serve warm.

1 biscuit: 153 cal., 7g fat (4g sat. fat), 18mg chol., 437mg sod., 20g carb. (1g sugars, 1g fiber), 3g pro.

CITRUS AVOCADO SPINACH SALAD

CITRUS AVOCADO SPINACH SALAD

Tossing this salad together with creamy avocado and tangy citrus is so simple—and you don't even need to peel the oranges.

—Karole Friemann,
Kimberling City, MO

- -

Takes: 15 min. • **Makes:** 8 servings

- 8 **cups fresh baby spinach (about 6 oz.)**
- 3 **cups refrigerated citrus salad, drained**
- 2 **medium ripe avocados, peeled and sliced**
- 1 **cup crumbled blue cheese**
  Optional: Toasted sliced almonds and salad dressing of your choice

Divide spinach among 8 plates; top with the citrus salad and avocados. Sprinkle with the blue cheese and, if desired, dressing and almonds. Serve immediately.

Notes: This recipe was tested with Del Monte SunFresh Citrus Salad. To toast nuts, bake in a shallow pan in a 350° oven for 5-10 minutes or cook in a skillet over low heat until lightly browned, stirring occasionally.

1 serving: 168 cal., 10g fat (4g sat. fat), 13mg chol., 231mg sod., 16g carb. (10g sugars, 3g fiber), 5g pro.

GRANDMOTHER'S ORANGE SALAD

STOVETOP MACARONI & CHEESE

When I was a girl, Mama used Texas Longhorn cheese in this recipe. After it melted all over the macaroni, I loved to dig in and see how many strings of cheese would follow my spoonful.

—Imogene Hutton, Brownwood, TX

- -

Takes: 25 min.
Makes: 6 servings

1	pkg. (7 oz.) elbow macaroni
¼	cup butter, cubed
¼	cup all-purpose flour
½	tsp. salt
	Dash pepper
2	cups 2% milk
8	oz. sharp cheddar cheese, shredded
	Paprika, optional

1. Cook macaroni according to package directions. Meanwhile, in a large saucepan, melt butter over medium heat. Stir in flour, salt and pepper until smooth; gradually whisk in milk. Bring to a boil; stir constantly. Cook and stir 1-2 minutes longer or until thickened.

2. Stir in cheese until melted. Drain macaroni; add to cheese sauce and stir to coat. If desired, sprinkle with paprika.

1 cup: 388 cal., 22g fat (15g sat. fat), 72mg chol., 542mg sod., 33g carb. (5g sugars, 1g fiber), 16g pro.

Swiss Mac & Cheese: Saute ⅓ cup chopped onion in ⅓ cup melted butter; add flour and proceed as directed. Substitute Swiss cheese for cheddar and add ⅛ tsp. nutmeg.

GRANDMOTHER'S ORANGE SALAD

This slightly sweet gelatin salad is a little bit tangy, too. It adds beautiful color to any meal and appeals to all ages.

—Ann Eastman, Santa Monica, CA

- -

Prep: 20 min. + chilling
Makes: 10 servings

1	can (11 oz.) mandarin oranges
1	can (8 oz.) crushed pineapple
	Water
1	pkg. (6 oz.) orange gelatin
1	pint orange sherbet, softened
2	bananas, sliced

1. Drain oranges and pineapple, reserving juices. Set oranges and pineapple aside. Add enough water to juices to measure 2 cups. Place in a saucepan and bring to a boil; pour over gelatin in a large bowl. Stir until gelatin is dissolved. Stir in sherbet until smooth.

2. Chill until mixture is partially set (watch carefully). Fold in oranges, pineapple and bananas. Pour into an oiled 6-cup mold. Chill until firm.

1 serving: 161 cal., 1g fat (0 sat. fat), 2mg chol., 55mg sod., 39g carb. (35g sugars, 1g fiber), 2g pro.

STOVETOP MACARONI
& CHEESE

GARLIC MASHED CAULIFLOWER

I order cauliflower mash every time we visit our favorite restaurant. One night, I figured out how to make it at home and couldn't believe how easy it was. Lucky us!
—Barry Keiser, West Chester, PA

Takes: 25 min. • **Makes:** 4 servings

- 5 cups fresh cauliflowerets
- 1 garlic clove, thinly sliced
- 3 Tbsp. fat-free milk
- 3 Tbsp. reduced-fat mayonnaise
- ½ tsp. salt
- ⅛ tsp. white pepper
  Optional: Cracked black pepper and minced fresh chives

1. Place 1 in. of water in a large saucepan; add cauliflower and garlic. Bring to a boil. Reduce heat; simmer, covered, until tender, 10-15 minutes, stirring occasionally. Drain the garlic and cauliflower; return to pan.

2. Mash the cauliflower mixture to desired consistency. Stir in milk, mayonnaise, salt and white pepper. If desired, sprinkle with cracked pepper and chives.

½ cup: 74 cal., 4g fat (1g sat. fat), 4mg chol., 428mg sod., 8g carb. (4g sugars, 3g fiber), 3g pro. **Diabetic exchanges:** 1 vegetable, 1 fat.

PROSCIUTTO & PEAS

This peas and prosciutto dish has a delicious, slightly salty flavor. Even the pea-haters will like this one!
—Ann R. Sheehy, Lawrence, MA

Takes: 20 min. • **Makes:** 4 servings

- 1 Tbsp. olive oil
- 4 to 8 thin slices prosciutto, julienned
- ½ cup sliced fresh shiitake mushrooms
- 2 cups frozen peas, thawed
- 1 small onion, chopped

In a large cast-iron or other heavy skillet, heat oil over medium heat. Add prosciutto; cook until crisp, stirring occasionally. Remove with a slotted spoon; drain on paper towels. Cook and stir mushrooms, peas and onion in drippings until tender, 5-7 minutes. Sprinkle with the prosciutto.

¾ cup: 122 cal., 5g fat (1g sat. fat), 13mg chol., 349mg sod., 11g carb. (4g sugars, 4g fiber), 8g pro.

PROSCIUTTO & PEAS

CREAM CHEESE MASHED POTATOES

When I serve these potatoes, the bowl is always scraped clean. Before a big feast, I make them early and keep them warm in a slow cooker so I can focus on last-minute details.

—Jill Thomas, Washington, IN

- -

Prep: 20 min. • **Cook:** 15 min.
Makes: 20 servings

- 8 **lbs. russet potatoes**
- 1 **pkg. (8 oz.) cream cheese, softened**
- ½ **cup butter, melted**
- 2 **tsp. salt**
- ¾ **tsp. pepper**
  Additional melted butter, optional
- ¼ **cup finely chopped green onions**

1. Peel and cube potatoes. Place in a large stockpot; add water to cover. Bring to a boil. Reduce heat; cook potatoes, uncovered, until tender, 12-15 minutes. Drain.

2. With a mixer, beat cream cheese, ½ cup melted butter, salt and pepper until smooth. Add the potatoes; beat until light and fluffy. If desired, top with additional melted butter. Sprinkle with green onions.

¾ cup: 185 cal., 9g fat (5g sat. fat), 25mg chol., 318mg sod., 25g carb. (2g sugars, 2g fiber), 3g pro.

BAKED BUTTERNUT SQUASH

Lightly sweetened with nutmeg, cinnamon, butter and brown sugar, this easy butternut squash recipe offers plenty of harvest-fresh flavor.

—Heidi Vawdrey, Riverton, UT

- -

Prep: 10 min. • **Bake:** 1 hour
Makes: 6 servings

¼ tsp. salt
⅛ tsp. ground cinnamon
⅛ tsp. ground nutmeg
⅛ tsp. pepper
1 small butternut squash (about 2 lbs.)
2 Tbsp. butter, melted
6 tsp. brown sugar, divided

1. Preheat oven to 350°. Mix the seasoning ingredients. Halve the squash lengthwise; remove and discard seeds. Place squash in an 11x7-in. baking dish coated with cooking spray. Brush with melted butter; sprinkle with seasonings.
2. Place 2 tsp. brown sugar in the cavity of each squash half. Sprinkle the remaining brown sugar over the cut surfaces.
3. Bake, covered for 40 minutes. Uncover; bake until squash is tender, about another 20 minutes.
1 serving: 120 cal., 4g fat (2g sat. fat), 10mg chol., 136mg sod., 22g carb. (9g sugars, 5g fiber), 2g pro.
Diabetic exchanges: 1½ starch, ½ fat.

GARLIC KNOTS

Here's a handy bread that can be made in no time flat. Refrigerated biscuits make preparation simple. The classic Italian flavors complement a variety of meals.

—Jane Paschke, University Park, FL

- -

Takes: 30 min. • **Makes:** 2½ dozen

1   **tube (12 oz.) refrigerated buttermilk biscuits**
¼   **cup canola oil**
3   **Tbsp. grated Parmesan cheese**
1   **tsp. garlic powder**
1   **tsp. dried oregano**
1   **tsp. dried parsley flakes**

1. Preheat oven to 400°. Cut each biscuit into thirds. Roll each piece into a 4-in. rope and tie into a knot; tuck ends under. Place 2 in. apart on a greased baking sheet. Bake until golden brown, 8-10 minutes.
2. In a large bowl, combine the remaining ingredients; add the warm knots and gently toss to coat.
1 knot: 46 cal., 2g fat (0 sat. fat), 0 chol., 105mg sod., 6g carb. (0 sugars, 0 fiber), 1g pro.

TEST KITCHEN TIP
Melted butter (or a blend of olive oil and melted butter) would be a tasty substitution for canola oil in this recipe.

GARLIC KNOTS

PLANTAIN
FRITTERS

PLANTAIN FRITTERS

These golden brown plantain fritters are a favorite in West Africa, where my aunt served as a missionary for 45 years. Make sure the plantains are very ripe. You can substitute bananas if you'd like.

—Heather Ewald, Bothell, WA

- -

Takes: 20 min. • **Makes:** 2 dozen

- 2 **large ripe plantains or bananas, peeled**
- 1 **cup self-rising flour**
- 1 **small onion, cut into wedges**
- ¼ **tsp. salt**
-    **Dash pepper**
-    **Oil for deep-fat frying**

1. Place ripe plantains in a food processor; cover and process until smooth. Add the flour, onion, salt and pepper; cover and process until blended (batter will be moist).

2. In an electric skillet or deep-fat fryer, heat ¼ in. of oil to 375°. Drop tablespoons of batter, a few at a time, into hot oil. Cook until golden brown, 1 minute on each side. Drain on paper towels.

Note: As a substitute for 1 cup of self-rising flour, place 1½ tsp. baking powder and ½ tsp. salt in a measuring cup. Add enough all-purpose flour to measure 1 cup.

1 fritter: 77 cal., 5g fat (0 sat. fat), 0 chol., 87mg sod., 9g carb. (2g sugars, 1g fiber), 1g pro.

PINA COLADA CARROT SALAD

PINA COLADA CARROT SALAD

This sweet carrot salad, with pina colada yogurt, macadamia nuts and green grapes, has a tropical theme. Just mix and chill out.

—Emily Tyra, Lake Ann, MI

- -

Takes: 10 min. • **Makes:** 4 servings

- 1 **pkg. (10 oz.) julienned carrots**
- 1 **cup green grapes, halved**
- ¾ **cup pina colada yogurt**
- ⅓ **cup salted dry roasted macadamia nuts, chopped**
-    **Lemon wedges**

In a large bowl, combine carrots, grapes, yogurt and macadamia nuts; toss to coat. Squeeze lemon wedges over salad before serving.

¾ cup: 184 cal., 9g fat (2g sat. fat), 2mg chol., 157mg sod., 24g carb. (19g sugars, 3g fiber), 3g pro.
Diabetic exchanges: 1½ fat, 1 starch, 1 vegetable.

PRESSURE-COOKER BUFFALO WING POTATOES

PRESSURE-COOKER BUFFALO WING POTATOES

I was getting tired of mashed potatoes and baked spuds, so I decided to create something new. This potluck-ready recipe is an easy and delicious twist on the usual potato dish.

—Summer Feaker, Ankeny, IA

- -

Takes: 20 min. • **Makes:** 6 servings

2 **lbs. Yukon Gold potatoes, cut into 1-in. cubes**

1 **small sweet yellow pepper, chopped**
½ **small red onion, chopped**
¼ **cup Buffalo wing sauce**
½ **cup shredded cheddar cheese**
   Optional toppings: Crumbled cooked bacon, sliced green onions and sour cream

1. Place steamer basket and 1 cup water in a 6-qt. electric pressure cooker. Set potatoes, yellow pepper and onion in basket. Lock lid; close the pressure-release valve. Adjust to pressure-cook on high for 3 minutes. Quick-release pressure.

2. Remove vegetables to a serving bowl; discard cooking liquid. Add Buffalo wing sauce to vegetables; gently stir to coat. Sprinkle with cheese. Cover and let stand until cheese is melted, 1-2 minutes. If desired, top with bacon, green onions and sour cream.

¾ cup: 182 cal., 4g fat (2g sat. fat), 9mg chol., 382mg sod., 32g carb. (3g sugars, 3g fiber), 6g pro. **Diabetic exchanges:** 2 starch, ½ fat.

CREAMY SKILLET NOODLES WITH PEAS

I've made this creamy noodle side for years. Since kids and adults go for it, I keep these ingredients on hand at all times.
—Anita Groff, Perkiomenville, PA

- -

Takes: 25 min. • **Makes:** 6 servings

- ¼ cup butter, cubed
- 2 Tbsp. canola oil
- 5 cups uncooked fine egg noodles
- 2½ cups frozen peas (about 10 oz.)
- 2½ cups chicken broth
- 1 cup half-and-half cream
- ½ tsp. salt
- ¼ tsp. pepper

In a large skillet, heat butter and oil over medium heat. Add noodles; cook and stir 2-3 minutes or until lightly browned. Stir in peas, broth, cream, salt and pepper. Bring to a boil. Reduce heat; simmer, covered, 10-12 minutes or until noodles are tender, stirring occasionally.

¾ cup: 329 cal., 31g fat (8g sat. fat), 76mg chol., 757mg sod., 31g carb. (6g sugars, 4g fiber), 9g pro.

CREAMY SKILLET NOODLES WITH PEAS

PEAR & BLUE CHEESE SALAD

This crisp fall salad gets its tartness from fresh pears, an extra crunch from pecans and a hint of creaminess from blue cheese. It's simple, but always impresses.
—*Taste of Home* Test Kitchen

- -

Takes: 10 min. • **Makes:** 10 servings

- 12 cups torn romaine
- ⅔ cup balsamic vinaigrette
- 2 medium pears, sliced
- ⅔ cup crumbled blue cheese
- ⅔ cup glazed pecans

Place romaine in a large bowl. Drizzle leaves with vinaigrette; toss to coat. Top with pears, cheese and pecans. Serve immediately.

1 cup: 133 cal., 8g fat (2g sat. fat), 7mg chol., 324mg sod., 12g carb. (8g sugars, 3g fiber), 3g pro.
Diabetic exchanges: 1½ fat, 1 vegetable, ½ starch.

SKILLET MAC & CHEESE

This creamy mac and cheese is so simple it's almost too easy! Kids always go for the rich cheese flavor, but I've never met an adult who didn't love it just as much.

—Ann Bowers, Rockport, TX

- -

Takes: 25 min. • **Makes:** 4 servings

- 2 cups uncooked pasta (about 8 oz.), such as elbow macaroni, cavatappi or shells
- 2 Tbsp. butter
- 2 Tbsp. all-purpose flour
- 1½ cups half-and-half cream
- ¾ lb. Velveeta, cubed
  Optional toppings: Fresh arugula, halved cherry tomatoes and coarsely ground pepper

1. Cook macaroni according to package directions; drain.
2. Meanwhile, in a large cast-iron or other heavy skillet, melt butter over medium heat. Stir in flour until smooth; gradually whisk in cream. Bring to a boil, stirring constantly. Cook and stir until thickened, about 2 minutes. Reduce heat; stir in the cheese until melted.
3. Add macaroni; cook and stir until heated through. Top as desired.
1½ cups: 600 cal., 37g fat (23g sat. fat), 144mg chol., 1185mg sod., 40g carb. (9g sugars, 1g fiber), 23g pro.

INSALATA CAPRESE

INSALATA CAPRESE

*The colors in a classic Caprese
salad resemble the Italian flag.
For extra zing, I like to add a
splash of balsamic vinegar.*
—Joe Colamonico,
North Charleston, SC

- -

Takes: 25 min. • **Makes:** 8 servings

2½ lbs. plum tomatoes
(about 10), cut into
1-in. pieces
1 carton (8 oz.) fresh
mozzarella cheese pearls
½ cup pitted ripe olives
3 Tbsp. olive oil
¼ cup thinly sliced fresh basil
2 tsp. minced fresh oregano
½ tsp. salt
¼ tsp. pepper
Balsamic vinegar, optional

In a large bowl, mix tomatoes, cheese
pearls and olives. Drizzle with the oil.
Sprinkle with basil, oregano, salt and
pepper; toss to coat. Let salad stand
10 minutes before serving. If desired,
drizzle with vinegar.

¾ cup: 160 cal., 12g fat (5g sat. fat),
22mg chol., 257mg sod., 7g carb. (4g
sugars, 2g fiber), 6g pro.

★ ★ ★ ★ ★ **READER REVIEW**

"Just perfect! I used
cherry tomatoes and
cut them in half. I
did add the balsamic
vinegar, and it was
so good with the
fresh herbs."
—DEBORAHLZ, TASTEOFHOME.COM

CHEDDAR CORN DOG MUFFINS

wire rack. Serve muffins warm. Refrigerate leftover muffins.
Freeze option: Freeze cooled muffins in freezer containers. To use, microwave each muffin on high until heated through, 30-60 seconds.
1 muffin: 216 cal., 10g fat (4g sat. fat), 46mg chol., 619mg sod., 23g carb. (7g sugars, 2g fiber), 8g pro.

CREAMY JALAPENO CORN

My version of creamed corn gets a spicy kick from jalapeno peppers. Try a chopped poblano or small red bell pepper for a more mild side dish.

—Judy Carty, Wichita, KS

- -

Prep: 15 min. • **Cook:** 4 hours
Makes: 8 servings

- 2 pkg. (16 oz. each) frozen corn
- 1 pkg. (8 oz.) cream cheese, softened and cubed
- 4 jalapeno peppers, seeded and finely chopped
- ¼ cup butter, cubed
- 2 Tbsp. water
- ½ tsp. salt
- ¼ tsp. pepper

In a 3-qt. slow cooker, combine all ingredients. Cover and cook on low until corn is tender, stirring occasionally, 4-5 hours.
Note: Wear disposable gloves when cutting hot peppers; the oils can burn skin. Avoid touching your face.
¾ cup: 251 cal., 16g fat (10g sat. fat), 46mg chol., 275mg sod., 25g carb. (2g sugars, 3g fiber), 6g pro.

CHEDDAR CORN DOG MUFFINS

I wanted a change from basic hot dogs, so I made corn dog muffins. I added jalapenos to this kid-friendly recipe and that won my husband over, too.

—Becky Tarala, Palm Coast, FL

- -

Takes: 25 min. • **Makes:** 9 muffins

- 1 pkg. (8½ oz.) cornbread/ muffin mix
- ⅔ cup 2% milk
- 1 large egg, lightly beaten, room temperature
- 5 turkey hot dogs, sliced
- ½ cup shredded sharp cheddar cheese
- 2 Tbsp. finely chopped pickled jalapeno, optional

1. Preheat oven to 400°. Line 9 muffin cups with foil liners or grease 9 nonstick muffin cups.
2. In a small bowl, combine muffin mix, milk and egg; stir in hot dogs, cheese and, if desired, jalapeno. Fill prepared cups three-fourths full.
3. Bake until a toothpick inserted in the center comes out clean, 14-18 minutes. Cool 5 minutes before removing from pan to a

CREAMY JALAPENO
CORN

CHEESY MASHED POTATO CUPS

This recipe gives you an extra batch of potato cups to freeze. They're a nice alternative to the standard side dish of potatoes or rice.

—Jill Hancock, Nashua, NH

- -

Prep: 40 min. • **Bake:** 15 min.
Makes: 2 pans (6 servings each)

3½ lbs. cubed peeled potatoes
½ cup 2% milk
¼ cup butter
1 tsp. salt
⅛ tsp. pepper
1⅓ cups plus 2 Tbsp. shredded Colby-Monterey Jack cheese, divided
2 tsp. dried parsley flakes

1. Place potatoes in a large saucepan and cover with water. Bring to a boil. Reduce the heat; cover and cook for 10-15 minutes or until tender. Drain.
2. In a large bowl, mash potatoes, milk, butter, salt and pepper until smooth. Stir in 1⅓ cups cheese. Grease two 6-portion muffin pans; divide potato mixture between pans. Sprinkle with remaining cheese; top with parsley.
3. Cover and freeze 1 pan for up to 3 months. Bake the second pan, uncovered, at 350° until heated through and the cheese is melted, 15-20 minutes.
To use frozen potato cups: Thaw in the refrigerator. Bake as directed.
1 potato cup: 202 cal., 8g fat (6g sat. fat), 23mg chol., 322mg sod., 28g carb. (2g sugars, 2g fiber), 6g pro.

CORN FRITTER PATTIES

These five-ingredient fritters are a thrifty way to enjoy a staple of southern cooking without having to leave home.

—Megan Hamilton, Pineville, MO

- -

Takes: 30 min. • **Makes:** 4 servings

1 cup pancake mix
1 large egg, lightly beaten
¼ cup plus 2 Tbsp. 2% milk
1 can (7 oz.) whole kernel corn, drained
Canola oil

1. In a small bowl, combine the pancake mix, egg and milk just until moistened. Stir in the corn.
2. In a cast-iron or electric skillet, heat ¼ in. oil to 375°. Drop batter by ¼ cupfuls into oil; press lightly to flatten. Cook until golden brown, about 2 minutes on each side.
2 fritters: 228 cal., 11g fat (1g sat. fat), 48mg chol., 590mg sod., 26g carb. (5g sugars, 3g fiber), 6g pro.

CORN FRITTER PATTIES

**BUTTERY
CARROTS**

BUTTERY CARROTS

*My mother made this recipe
often when I was growing up.
She got it from a friend who was
a chef at a local restaurant my
parents frequented. The onions
really bring out the sweetness of
the carrots. When I have carrots
fresh from the garden, I don't
even peel them—I just scrub
them well before cutting. For
holiday buffets, I often double
or triple this recipe.*

—Mary Ellen Chambers,
Lakewood, OH

- -

Takes: 20 min. • **Makes:** 12 servings

3   **lbs. medium carrots, halved
     crosswise and cut into strips**
2   **medium onions,
     halved and thinly sliced**
½   **cup butter, melted**
½   **cup chopped fresh parsley**
½   **tsp. salt**
     **Coarsely ground pepper,
     optional**

1. Fill 6-qt. stockpot with 2 in. water.
Add the carrots and onions; bring to
a boil. Reduce heat; simmer, covered,
until the carrots are crisp-tender,
10-12 minutes.
2. Drain vegetables. Toss with
remaining ingredients.

¾ cup: 123 cal., 8g fat (5g sat. fat),
20mg chol., 240mg sod., 13g carb.
(6g sugars, 4g fiber), 1g pro.

TEST KITCHEN TIP
To keep parsley fresh for
up to a month, trim the
ends of the stems and
place the bunch in a
tumbler with an inch of
water. Be sure no loose
leaves are in the water. Tie
a produce bag around the
tumbler to trap humidity;
store in the refrigerator.

RANCH POTATO SALAD

RANCH POTATO SALAD

I make this creamy potato salad with cheese, bacon and ranch salad dressing. My sister asked for the recipe as soon as she tried it.

—Lynn Breunig, Wind Lake, WI

- -

Prep: 30 min. + chilling
Makes: 8 servings

2 **lbs. red potatoes**
1 **bottle (8 oz.) ranch salad dressing**
1 **cup shredded cheddar cheese**
1 **pkg. (2.8 oz.) bacon bits**
¼ **tsp. pepper**
   Dash garlic powder

1. Scrub potatoes; place them in a large saucepan and cover with water. Bring to a boil. Reduce the heat; cover and simmer until tender, 20-25 minutes.

2. In a large bowl, combine the remaining ingredients (dressing will be thick). Drain potatoes and cut into cubes; add to the dressing and gently toss to coat. Cover and refrigerate for 2 hours or until chilled. Refrigerate leftovers.

1 cup: 316 cal., 22g fat (6g sat. fat), 27mg chol., 649mg sod., 20g carb. (2g sugars, 2g fiber), 9g pro.

CHEESY BACON SPAGHETTI SQUASH

This quick casserole is called cheesy for a reason. Stir in any kind you've got.

—Jean Williams, Stillwater, OK

- -

Takes: 30 min. • **Makes:** 4 servings

- 1 **large spaghetti squash (3½ lbs.)**
- 4 **bacon strips, chopped**
- 3 **Tbsp. butter**
- 1 **Tbsp. brown sugar**
- ½ **tsp. salt**
- ¼ **tsp. pepper**
- ½ **cup shredded Swiss cheese**

1. Halve squash lengthwise; discard seeds. Place squash on a microwave-safe plate, cut side down; microwave on high until tender, 15-20 minutes. Cool slightly. Separate strands with a fork.

2. In a large skillet, cook bacon over medium heat until crisp, stirring occasionally. With a slotted spoon, remove bacon to paper towels; reserve drippings.

3. In same pan, heat drippings over medium heat; stir in butter, brown sugar, salt and pepper until blended. Add squash; toss and heat through. Remove from heat; stir in cheese. Top with bacon.

1 cup: 381 cal., 26g fat (12g sat. fat), 54mg chol., 627mg sod., 32g carb. (4g sugars, 6g fiber), 10g pro.

CHEESY BACON SPAGHETTI SQUASH

SLOW-COOKED POTATOES WITH SPRING ONIONS

SLOW-COOKED POTATOES WITH SPRING ONIONS

I love the simplicity of this recipe, as well as the ease of preparation with my slow cooker. Everyone always likes roasted potatoes, even my pickiest child! Top with shredded or crumbled cheese, if you'd like.

—Theresa Gomez, Stuart, FL

- -

Prep: 5 min. • **Cook:** 6 hours
Makes: 12 servings

- 4 lbs. small red potatoes
- 8 green onions, chopped (about 1 cup)
- 1 cup chopped sweet onion
- ¼ cup olive oil
- ½ tsp. salt
- ½ tsp. pepper

In a 5- or 6-qt. slow cooker, combine all ingredients. Cook, covered, on low until the potatoes are tender, 6-8 hours.

1 serving: 157 cal., 5g fat (1g sat. fat), 0 chol., 110mg sod., 26g carb. (2g sugars, 3g fiber), 3g pro.
Diabetic exchanges: 1½ starch, 1 fat.

BROCCOLI WITH GARLIC, BACON & PARMESAN

My approach to broccoli is to cook it slowly in broth so the garlic blends with smoky bacon. A few simple ingredients make ordinary broccoli irresistible.

—Erin Chilcoat, Central Islip, NY

- -

Takes: 30 min. • **Makes:** 8 servings

BROCCOLI WITH GARLIC, BACON & PARMESAN

- 1 tsp. salt
- 2 bunches broccoli (about 3 lbs.), stems removed, cut into florets
- 6 thick-sliced bacon strips, chopped
- 2 Tbsp. olive oil
- 6 to 8 garlic cloves, thinly sliced
- ½ tsp. crushed red pepper flakes
- ¼ cup shredded Parmesan cheese

1. Fill a 6-qt. stockpot two-thirds full with water; add salt and bring to a boil over high heat. In batches, add broccoli and cook until broccoli turns bright green, 2-3 minutes; remove with a slotted spoon.

2. In a large skillet, cook bacon over medium heat until crisp, stirring occasionally. Remove with a slotted spoon; drain on paper towels. Discard drippings, reserving 1 Tbsp. in pan.

3. Add oil to drippings; heat over medium heat. Add garlic and pepper flakes; cook and stir until garlic is fragrant, 2-3 minutes (do not allow to brown). Add broccoli; cook until broccoli is tender, stirring occasionally. Stir in bacon; sprinkle with cheese.

¾ cup: 155 cal., 10g fat (3g sat. fat), 11mg chol., 371mg sod., 11g carb. (3g sugars, 4g fiber), 8g pro.
Diabetic exchanges: 2 fat, 1 vegetable.

HOMEMADE
FRY BREAD

HOMEMADE FRY BREAD

Crispy, doughy and totally delicious, this fry bread is fantastic with nearly any sweet or savory toppings you can think of. We love it with a little butter, a drizzle of honey and a squeeze of lemon.

—Thelma Tyler, Dragoon, AZ

- -

Prep: 20 min. + standing
Cook: 15 min. • **Makes:** 12 servings

2 cups unbleached flour
½ cup nonfat dry milk powder
3 tsp. baking powder
½ tsp. salt
4½ tsp. shortening
⅔ to ¾ cup water
Oil for deep-fat frying
Optional: Butter, honey and lemon juice

1. Combine flour, dry milk powder, baking powder and salt; cut in the shortening until crumbly. Add water gradually, mixing to form a firm ball. Divide dough; shape into 12 balls. Let stand, covered, for 10 minutes. Roll each ball into a 6-in. circle. With a sharp knife, cut a ½-in.-diameter hole in center of each.

2. In a large cast-iron skillet, heat oil over medium-high heat. Fry dough circles, 1 at a time, until puffed and golden, about 1 minute on each side. Drain on paper towels; if desired, serve warm with butter, honey and fresh lemon juice.

1 piece: 124 cal., 5g fat (1g sat. fat), 1mg chol., 234mg sod., 17g carb. (2g sugars, 1g fiber), 3g pro.

STRAWBERRY FETA TOSSED SALAD

A neighbor served this light salad at a summer barbecue. I've since tried it with many ingredient combinations, but this one draws the most compliments.
—Lisa Lesinski-Topp, Menomonee Falls, WI

- -

Takes: 10 min. • **Makes:** 6 servings

- 6 **cups torn mixed salad greens**
- 2 **cups fresh strawberries, sliced**
- 1 **pkg. (4 oz.) crumbled feta cheese**
- ¼ **cup sunflower kernels**
  Balsamic vinaigrette

Place first 4 ingredients in a large bowl. To serve, drizzle with vinaigrette; toss to combine.

1 cup: 103 cal., 6g fat (2g sat. fat), 10mg chol., 259mg sod., 8g carb. (3g sugars, 3g fiber), 6g pro.

★ ★ ★ ★ ★ **READER REVIEW**
"We enjoyed this very summery salad! I added some minced fresh dill and next time I will add some scallion or sweet onion because we enjoy the taste. Used white balsamic vinegar dressing. Good!"
—ANNRMS, TASTEOFHOME.COM

STRAWBERRY FETA TOSSED SALAD

MARINATED ASPARAGUS WITH BLUE CHEESE

Asparagus marinated in vinaigrette and dotted with cheese makes an awesome side. We're blue cheese fans, but you might like Parmesan or feta.
—Susan Vaith, Jacksonville, FL

- -

Prep: 20 min. + marinating
Makes: 4 servings

- 1 **lb. fresh asparagus, trimmed**
- 4 **green onions, thinly sliced**
- ¼ **cup olive oil**
- 2 **Tbsp. white wine vinegar**
- 1 **garlic clove, minced**
- ½ **tsp. salt**
- ¼ **tsp. pepper**
- ½ **cup crumbled blue cheese**

1. In a large saucepan, bring 6 cups water to a boil. Add asparagus; cook, uncovered, 2-3 minutes or just until crisp-tender. Remove asparagus and immediately drop into ice water. Drain and pat dry.
2. In a bowl or shallow dish, combine green onions, oil, vinegar, garlic, salt and pepper. Add asparagus and turn to coat. Cover; refrigerate 1 hour.
3. Drain asparagus, discarding marinade. Place asparagus on a serving plate; sprinkle with cheese.
1 serving: 136 cal., 12g fat (4g sat. fat), 13mg chol., 348mg sod., 3g carb. (1g sugars, 1g fiber), 5g pro.

SOUPS & SANDWICHES

1

2

SWEET & SPICY PINEAPPLE CHICKEN SANDWICHES P.113

3

4

5

DISCOVER A PERFECT PAIRING OF TASTY LUNCHTIME STAPLES, EACH PREPARED WITH FIVE INGREDIENTS OR FEWER.

CHEESY
WILD RICE
SOUP

CHEESY WILD RICE SOUP

We often eat easy-to-make soups when there's not a lot of time to cook. I replaced the wild rice in the original recipe with a boxed rice mix. This creamy concoction is now a favorite.

—Lisa Hofer, Hitchcock, SD

- -

Takes: 30 min.
Makes: 8 servings (2 qt.)

- 1   pkg. (6.2 oz.) fast-cooking long grain and wild rice mix
- 4   cups 2% milk
- 1   can (10¾ oz.) condensed cream of potato soup, undiluted
- 8   oz. Velveeta, cubed
- ½   lb. bacon strips, cooked and crumbled
     Optional: Minced chives and oyster crackers

In a large saucepan, prepare rice mix according to package directions. Add the milk, soup and cheese. Cook and stir until cheese is melted. Garnish with bacon and, if desired, minced fresh chives and oyster crackers.

1 cup: 464 cal., 29g fat (14g sat. fat), 70mg chol., 1492mg sod., 29g carb. (9g sugars, 1g fiber), 21g pro.

★ ★ ★ ★ ★ **READER REVIEW**

"This recipe was so good that my 7-year-old daughter wanted some of the leftovers for breakfast the next morning!"

—SLBASTRESS, TASTEOFHOME.COM

MUSHROOM PEAR MELTS

MUSHROOM PEAR MELTS

I really like mushrooms with cheese. Add pears, broil away, and you have a scrumptious open-faced sandwich. Serve with a salad and fruity tea.

—Marla Hyatt, St. Paul, MN

- -

Takes: 25 min. • **Makes:** 4 servings

- 2   Tbsp. butter
- 4   cups sliced fresh shiitake or baby portobello mushrooms (about 10 oz.)
- ½   tsp. salt
- ¼   tsp. pepper
- 8   slices whole wheat bread, toasted
- 2   large ripe Bosc pears, thinly sliced
- 8   slices provolone cheese

1. Preheat broiler. In a large cast-iron or other heavy skillet, heat butter over medium-high heat. Add the mushrooms; cook and stir until tender, 5-7 minutes. Stir in salt and pepper.
2. Place toast slices on a rack of a broiler pan. Top with mushrooms; layer with pears and cheese. Broil 3-4 in. from heat until cheese is lightly browned, 2-3 minutes.

2 open-faced sandwiches: 421 cal., 20g fat (11g sat. fat), 45mg chol., 883mg sod., 46g carb. (15g sugars, 9g fiber), 19g pro.

SAUSAGE & PEPPER SHEET-PAN SANDWICHES

Sausage with peppers was always on the table when I was growing up. Here's how to do it the easy way: Just grab a sheet pan and the ingredients, then let the oven do the work.
—Debbie Glasscock, Conway, AR

Prep: 20 min. • **Bake:** 30 min.
Makes: 6 servings

- 1 lb. uncooked sweet Italian turkey sausage links, roughly chopped
- 3 medium sweet red peppers, seeded and sliced
- 1 large onion, halved and sliced
- 1 Tbsp. olive oil
- 6 hot dog buns, split
- 6 slices provolone cheese

1. Preheat oven to 375°. Place the sausage pieces in a 15x10x1-in. sheet pan, arranging peppers and onion around sausage. Drizzle olive oil over sausage and vegetables; bake, stirring mixture after 15 minutes, until the sausage is no longer pink and the vegetables are tender, 30-35 minutes.
2. During the last 5 minutes of baking, arrange the buns cut side up in a second sheet pan; top each bun bottom with a cheese slice. Bake until the buns are golden brown and cheese is melted. Spoon sausage and pepper mixture onto bun bottoms. Replace tops.
1 sandwich: 315 cal., 15g fat (5g sat. fat), 43mg chol., 672mg sod., 28g carb. (7g sugars, 2g fiber), 18g pro.

SUPER-FAST MEXICAN SOUP

We like to take this spicy soup to rodeos on cool nights or sip it by a campfire. For toppings, try onions, avocado, sour cream, jalapenos, cheese and salsa.
—Gloria Huse, Simpsonville, SC

Takes: 25 min. • **Makes:** 4 servings

- 2 tsp. olive oil
- 1 lb. boneless skinless chicken thighs, cut into ¾-in. pieces
- 1 Tbsp. reduced-sodium taco seasoning
- 1 cup frozen corn
- 1 cup salsa
- 1 carton (32 oz.) reduced-sodium chicken broth

1. In a large saucepan, heat oil over medium-high heat. Add the chicken; cook and stir 6-8 minutes or until no longer pink. Stir in taco seasoning.
2. Add the remaining ingredients; bring to a boil. Reduce heat; simmer, uncovered, 5 minutes to allow the flavors to blend. Skim the fat before serving.
1½ cups: 254 cal., 11g fat (3g sat. fat), 76mg chol., 998mg sod., 14g carb. (5g sugars, 1g fiber), 25g pro.

SUPER-FAST MEXICAN SOUP

PULLED PORK
SANDWICHES

❄
PULLED PORK
SANDWICHES

*"Foolproof" is a perfect way
to describe my barbecue pork
recipe. With just four ingredients
and a slow cooker, you can make
these fabulous sandwiches with
very little effort.*

—Sarah Johnson, Chicago, IL

Prep: 15 min. • **Cook:** 7 hours
Makes: 6 servings

1   **lemon-garlic pork loin filet
    (about 1⅓ lbs.)**
1   **can (12 oz.) Dr Pepper**
1   **bottle (18 oz.) barbecue
    sauce**
6   **hamburger buns, split**

1. Place pork in a 3-qt. slow cooker.
Pour Dr Pepper over top. Cover and
cook on low until meat is tender,
7-9 hours.

2. Remove the meat; cool slightly.
Discard cooking juices. Shred meat
with 2 forks and return to slow
cooker. Stir in the barbecue sauce;
heat through. Serve on buns.

Freeze option: Place individual
portions of the cooled meat mixture
and juice in freezer containers. To
use, partially thaw in refrigerator
overnight. Microwave, covered, on
high in a microwave-safe dish until
heated through, stirring occasionally;
add water if necessary.

1 sandwich: 348 cal., 8g fat (2g sat.
fat), 45mg chol., 1695mg sod., 43g
carb. (22g sugars, 2g fiber), 25g pro.

SAUSAGE & SPINACH CALZONES

SAUSAGE & SPINACH CALZONES

These quick, comforting calzones are perfect for easy meals—or even a midnight snack. My co-workers always ask me to make them when it's my turn to bring in lunch.

—Kourtney Williams, Mechanicsville, VA

- -

Takes: 30 min. • **Makes:** 4 servings

½	**lb. bulk Italian sausage**
3	**cups fresh baby spinach**
1	**tube (13.8 oz.) refrigerated pizza crust**
¾	**cup shredded part-skim mozzarella cheese**
½	**cup part-skim ricotta cheese**
¼	**tsp. pepper**
	Pizza sauce, optional

1. Preheat oven to 400°. In a large skillet, cook and crumble sausage over medium heat until no longer pink, 4-6 minutes; drain. Add the spinach; cook and stir until wilted. Remove from heat.

2. On a lightly floured surface, unroll and pat the dough into a 15x11-in. rectangle. Cut into 4 rectangles. Sprinkle mozzarella cheese on half of each rectangle to within 1 in. of the edges.

3. Stir ricotta cheese and pepper into sausage mixture; spoon over mozzarella cheese. Fold dough over filling; press edges with a fork to seal. Place on a greased baking sheet.

4. Bake until light golden brown, 10-15 minutes. If desired, serve with pizza sauce.

Freeze option: Freeze the cooled calzones in airtight freezer container. To use, microwave calzones on high until heated through.

1 calzone: 489 cal., 22g fat (9g sat. fat), 54mg chol., 1242mg sod., 51g carb. (7g sugars, 2g fiber), 23g pro.

QUICK RAVIOLI & SPINACH SOUP

I love my Italian American traditions, but I never had time to make a classic Italian wedding soup. So I created this shortcut version with ravioli.

—Cynthia Bent, Newark, DE

- -

Takes: 25 min.
Makes: 6 servings (2½ qt.)

2 cartons (32 oz. each) chicken broth
¼ tsp. onion powder
   Dash pepper
1 pkg. (9 oz.) refrigerated small cheese ravioli
4 cups coarsely chopped fresh spinach (about 4 oz.)
3 cups shredded cooked chicken
   Grated Parmesan cheese, optional

In a large saucepan, combine the broth, onion powder and pepper; bring to a boil. Add ravioli; cook, uncovered, for 7-10 minutes or until tender. Add spinach and chicken during the last 3 minutes of cooking. If desired, serve with cheese.

1⅔ cups: 292 cal., 11g fat (3g sat. fat), 91mg chol., 1638mg sod., 19g carb. (2g sugars, 2g fiber), 28g pro.

★ ★ ★ ★ ★ **READER REVIEW**
"This was a quick and easy meal that tasted wonderful. My entire family thought it was great. It's a keeper."
—DEBBOGS, TASTEOFHOME.COM

QUICK RAVIOLI & SPINACH SOUP

GRANDMA'S TOMATO SOUP

GARLIC BREAD PIZZA SANDWICHES

I love inventing new ways to make grilled cheese sandwiches for my kids. This version tastes like pizza. Using frozen garlic bread is a timesaver.
—Courtney Stultz, Weir, KS

- -

Takes: 20 min. • **Makes:** 4 servings

  1   **pkg. (11¼ oz.) frozen garlic Texas toast**
  ¼   **cup pasta sauce**
  4   **slices provolone cheese**
 16   **slices pepperoni**
  8   **slices thinly sliced hard salami**
       Additional pasta sauce, warmed, optional

1. Preheat griddle over medium-low heat. Add the garlic toast; cook until bread is lightly browned, 3-4 minutes per side.
2. Spoon 1 Tbsp. sauce over each of 4 pieces of toast. Top with cheese, pepperoni, salami and remaining toast. Cook until crisp and cheese is melted, 3-5 minutes, turning as necessary. If desired, serve with additional sauce.

1 sandwich: 456 cal., 28g fat (10g sat. fat), 50mg chol., 1177mg sod., 36g carb. (4g sugars, 2g fiber), 19g pro.

GRANDMA'S TOMATO SOUP

This recipe is my grandmother's. Originally, she even made the tomato juice in it from scratch! Gram had this recipe cooking on the stove every time I visited her. She enjoyed making this tomato soup and other favorite dishes for family and friends, and she made everything with love.
—Gerri Sysun, Narragansett, RI

- -

Takes: 15 min. • **Makes:** 2 servings

  2   **Tbsp. butter**
  1   **Tbsp. all-purpose flour**
  2   **cups tomato juice**
  ½   **cup water**
  2   **Tbsp. sugar**
  ⅛   **tsp. salt**
  ¾   **cup cooked wide egg noodles**
       Chopped fresh parsley, optional

In a saucepan over medium heat, melt butter. Add flour; stir to form a smooth paste. Gradually add tomato juice and water, stirring constantly; bring to a boil. Cook and stir until thickened, about 2 minutes. Add sugar and salt. Stir in egg noodles and heat through. If desired, sprinkle with parsley.

1 cup: 259 cal., 12g fat (7g sat. fat), 44mg chol., 1144mg sod., 36g carb. (20g sugars, 1g fiber), 4g pro.

GARLIC BREAD
PIZZA SANDWICHES

PESTO HAMBURGERS

PESTO HAMBURGERS

Give an Italian twist to basic burgers by topping them with pesto, strips of roasted red peppers and mozzarella cheese.
—*Taste of Home* Test Kitchen

- -

Takes: 20 min. • **Makes:** 4 servings

- 1½ **lbs. ground beef**
- ⅛ **tsp. salt**
- ⅛ **tsp. pepper**
- 4 **slices part-skim mozzarella cheese**
- ½ **cup prepared pesto**
- ⅓ **cup roasted sweet red pepper strips**
- 4 **hamburger buns, split and toasted**

1. Shape beef into four ¾-in.-thick patties. Season with salt and pepper. In a large skillet, cook patties over medium heat until meat is no longer pink, about 5 minutes on each side.

2. Top each burger with a slice of cheese, 2 Tbsp. pesto and pepper strips. Reduce heat; cover and simmer until cheese is melted, about 2 minutes. Serve on buns.

1 burger: 716 cal., 45g fat (17g sat. fat), 161mg chol., 779mg sod., 25g carb. (3g sugars, 2g fiber), 51g pro.

BAKED BEAN CHILI

Who says a good chili has to simmer all day? This zippy chili, with a touch of sweetness from the baked beans, can be made on the spur of the moment. It's an excellent standby when guests drop by. Served with bread and a salad, it's a hearty dinner everyone raves about.
—Nancy Wall, Bakersfield, CA

- -

Takes: 30 min.
Makes: 24 servings (6 qt.)

- 2   **lbs. ground beef**
- 3   **cans (28 oz. each) baked beans**
- 1   **can (46 oz.) tomato juice**
- 1   **can (11½ oz.) V8 juice**
- 1   **envelope chili seasoning**
      Optional: Sour cream, shredded cheddar cheese and sliced jalapenos

In a Dutch oven, cook beef over medium heat until no longer pink; drain. Stir in remaining ingredients. Bring to a boil. Reduce heat; simmer, uncovered, for 10 minutes. Serve with the sour cream, cheese and jalapenos if desired .

1 cup: 189 cal., 6g fat (2g sat. fat), 30mg chol., 721mg sod., 23g carb. (2g sugars, 6g fiber), 13g pro.

ITALIAN GRILLED CHEESE SANDWICHES

I made up this recipe for the students in the foods and nutrition class I teach. The kids like it so much, they often go home and fix it for their families.
—Beth Hiott, York, SC

- -

Takes: 25 min. • **Makes:** 4 servings

- 8   **slices Italian bread**
- 4   **Tbsp. prepared pesto**
- 4   **slices provolone cheese**
- 4   **slices part-skim mozzarella cheese**
- 5   **tsp. olive oil**
      Marinara sauce warmed, optional

1. Spread 4 bread slices with pesto. Layer with the cheeses; top with remaining bread. Spread outsides of sandwiches with oil.
2. In a large skillet over medium heat, toast the sandwiches for 3-4 minutes on each side or until cheese is melted. Serve with marinara if desired.

1 sandwich: 445 cal., 27g fat (10g sat. fat), 35mg chol., 759mg sod., 32g carb. (1g sugars, 2g fiber), 20g pro.

BAKED BEAN CHILI

EASY
BUTTERNUT SQUASH
SOUP

EASY BUTTERNUT SQUASH SOUP

When the weather turns cold, get cozy with a bowl of this butternut squash soup. The cream adds richness, but if you're looking to cut calories, it can be omitted.
—*Taste of Home* Test Kitchen

- -

Takes: 30 min.
Makes: 9 servings (2¼ qt.)

1 Tbsp. olive oil
1 large onion, chopped
3 garlic cloves, minced
1 medium butternut squash (3 lbs.), peeled and cubed
4 cups vegetable broth
¾ tsp. salt
¼ tsp. pepper
½ cup heavy whipping cream
   Optional: Additional heavy whipping cream and crispy sage leaves

1. In a large saucepan, heat oil over medium heat. Add the onion; cook and stir until tender. Add the garlic; cook 1 minute longer.
2. Stir in the squash, broth, salt and pepper; bring to a boil. Reduce heat; simmer, covered, 10-15 minutes or until squash is tender. Puree soup using an immersion blender. Or cool slightly and puree soup in batches in a blender; return to pan. Add the cream; cook and stir until heated through. If desired, garnish with additional heavy whipping cream and crispy sage.

1 cup: 157 cal., 7g fat (4g sat. fat), 17mg chol., 483mg sod., 23g carb. (6g sugars, 6g fiber), 3g pro.

BUFFALO CHICKEN SLIDERS

❄️
BUFFALO CHICKEN SLIDERS

I got the idea for these sliders from my mom and dad, who'd made a similar recipe for a family get-together. To make it special, I sometimes use several types of Buffalo sauce and let my guests mix and match their favorites.

—Christina Addison, Blanchester, OH

- -

Prep: 20 min. • **Cook:** 3 hours
Makes: 6 servings

- 1 **lb. boneless skinless chicken breasts**
- 2 **Tbsp. plus ⅓ cup Louisiana-style hot sauce, divided**
- ¼ **tsp. pepper**
- ¼ **cup butter, cubed**
- ¼ **cup honey**
- 12 **Hawaiian sweet rolls, warmed**
  Optional: Lettuce leaves, sliced tomato, thinly sliced red onion and crumbled blue cheese

1. Place the chicken in a 3-qt. slow cooker. Toss with 2 Tbsp. hot sauce and pepper; cook, covered, on low 3-4 hours or until tender.

2. Remove chicken; discard cooking juices. In a small saucepan, combine butter, honey and remaining hot sauce; cook and stir over medium heat until blended. Shred chicken with 2 forks; stir into sauce and heat through. Serve on rolls with desired optional ingredients.

Freeze option: Freeze cooled chicken mixture in freezer containers. To use, partially thaw in the refrigerator overnight. Microwave, covered, on high in a microwave-safe dish until heated through, stirring occasionally; add water or broth if necessary.

2 sliders: 396 cal., 15g fat (8g sat. fat), 92mg chol., 873mg sod., 44g carb. (24g sugars, 2g fiber), 24g pro.

SPRING PEA
SOUP

SPRING PEA SOUP

Truly a soup for the pea lover, this recipe originated with an idea in an old cookbook about eating better to live longer. Sauteed potatoes add body to an easy soup with a good texture and superb pea flavor.

—Denise Patterson, Bainbridge, OH

- -

Prep: 10 min. • **Cook:** 30 min.
Makes: 6 servings

2 **cups cubed peeled potatoes**
2 **Tbsp. butter**
6 **cups chicken broth**
2 **cups fresh or frozen peas,
   thawed**
2 **Tbsp. minced chives
   Microgreens, optional**

1. In a large saucepan, saute potatoes in butter until lightly browned. Stir in the broth; bring to a boil. Reduce heat; cover and simmer until the potatoes are tender, 10-15 minutes. Add the peas; cook until peas are tender, 5-8 minutes. Cool slightly.
2. In a blender, process the soup in batches until smooth. Return all to the pan; heat through. Sprinkle with chives and, if desired, microgreens.
1 cup: 133 cal., 5g fat (2g sat. fat), 15mg chol., 1012mg sod., 18g carb. (4g sugars, 3g fiber), 5g pro.

**PIGS IN A
BLANKET**

PIGS IN A BLANKET

These baked hot dog sandwiches appeal to kids of all ages. Even my husband, Allan, admits to enjoying every bite! We like to dip them in a bit of ketchup and mustard.

—Linda Young, Longmont, CO

- -

Takes: 25 min. • **Makes:** 4 servings

1 **tube (8 oz.) refrigerated
   crescent rolls**
8 **hot dogs**
1 **large egg, lightly beaten**
1 **Tbsp. water
   Caraway seeds**

1. Preheat oven to 375°. Separate crescent dough into triangles. Place hot dogs at wide ends of triangles and roll up. Place on an ungreased baking sheet. Combine egg and water; brush over rolls. Sprinkle caraway over tops; press lightly into rolls.
2. Bake 12-15 minutes or until golden brown.
2 sandwiches: 516 cal, 39g fat (12g sat. fat), 97mg chol., 1365mg sod., 27g carb. (8g sugars, 0 fiber), 16g pro.

GREEN CHILE POSOLE

This recipe combines parts of my nanny's and my mother's recipes that I learned when I was very young. An optional sprinkling of queso fresco over the top is an absolute delight in my opinion.
—Jaime Love, Las Vegas, NV

- -

Prep: 10 min. • **Cook:** 4 hours
Makes: 6 servings (2 qt.)

1 pork tenderloin (1 lb.), cut into 1-in. pieces
2 cans (15 oz. each) hominy, rinsed and drained
1 can (4 oz.) chopped green chiles
¼ tsp. salt
¼ tsp. pepper
4 cups chicken broth, divided
3 tomatillos, husked and chopped
   Optional: Sliced avocado, lime wedge, sliced jalapenos, sliced radishes, chopped cilantro and sour cream

1. In a 3- or 4-qt. slow cooker, combine first 5 ingredients and 3¾ cups broth. Puree tomatillos with remaining broth in a blender; stir into pork mixture.
2. Cook, covered, on low until the pork is tender, 4-5 hours. Serve with avocado and other toppings as desired.
1⅓ cups: 173 cal., 3g fat (1g sat. fat), 46mg chol., 1457mg sod., 17g carb. (1g sugars, 4g fiber), 17g pro.

❄ GOURMET BARBECUE BEEF SANDWICHES

These beef sandwiches were a tradition in my family on winter vacations after a long day of snow skiing, but they're a hit any time we make them. Serving the beef on croissants with melty provolone cheese makes the sandwiches a little more special.
—Katie Anderson, Vancouver, WA

- -

Prep: 10 min. • **Cook:** 8 hours 5 min.
Makes: 12 servings

1 beef rump roast or bottom round roast (3 to 4 lbs.)
½ tsp. salt
¼ tsp. pepper
1 cup barbecue sauce
12 croissants, split
12 slices provolone cheese

Optional: Tomato slices, lettuce leaves and red onion slices

1. Rub roast with salt and pepper. Place in a 5- or 6-qt. slow cooker. Cook, covered, on low 8-10 hours or until meat is tender.
2. Remove roast; cool slightly. Skim fat from cooking juices. Slice beef; return beef and cooking juices to slow cooker. Add barbecue sauce; heat through. Place the croissant bottoms on a baking sheet; top with cheese. Broil 4-6 in. from heat until cheese is melted, 1-2 minutes. Top with the beef. If desired, serve with optional toppings. Replace the croissant tops.
1 sandwich: 511 cal., 25g fat (13g sat. fat), 125mg chol., 805mg sod., 38g carb. (15g sugars, 2g fiber), 33g pro.

GOURMET BARBECUE BEEF SANDWICHES

SWEET & SPICY PINEAPPLE CHICKEN SANDWICHES

❄ SWEET & SPICY PINEAPPLE CHICKEN SANDWICHES

My kids often ask for chicken sloppy joes, and this version has a bonus of sweet pineapple. It is a perfect recipe to double for a potluck. Try topping the easy sandwiches with some smoked Gouda cheese.

—Nancy Heishman, Las Vegas, NV

- -

Prep: 15 min. • **Cook:** 2¾ hours
Makes: 8 servings

2½ lbs. boneless skinless chicken breasts
1 bottle (18 oz.) sweet and spicy barbecue sauce, divided
2 Tbsp. honey mustard
1 can (8 oz.) unsweetened crushed pineapple, undrained
8 hamburger buns, split and toasted
Optional: Bibb lettuce leaves and thinly sliced red onion

1. Place the chicken breasts in a 4-qt. slow cooker. Combine ¼ cup barbecue sauce and mustard; pour over the chicken. Cover and cook on low 2½-3 hours or until the chicken is tender.

2. Remove the chicken; discard liquid. Shred chicken with 2 forks; return to slow cooker. Add crushed pineapple and remaining barbecue sauce; cover and cook on high for 15 minutes.

3. Serve on toasted buns with lettuce and onion if desired.

Freeze option: Place shredded chicken in freezer containers. Cool and freeze. To use, partially thaw in refrigerator overnight. Heat through in a covered saucepan, stirring gently; add broth if necessary.

1 sandwich: 415 cal., 6g fat (1g sat. fat), 78mg chol., 973mg sod., 56g carb. (30g sugars, 2g fiber), 34g pro.

TEST KITCHEN TIP
The chicken mixture is a bit more sweet than spicy. If your family likes things with more heat, simply add chopped jalapeno.

CHIPOTLE POMEGRANATE PULLED PORK

CHIPOTLE POMEGRANATE PULLED PORK

When I was making pulled pork and wanted to kick it up a bit, pomegranate jelly and smoky chipotles were the perfect addition. Yum!

—Tatiana Hendricks, Visalia, CA

- -

Prep: 10 min. • **Cook:** 8½ hours
Makes: 10 servings

- 1 **boneless pork shoulder butt roast (3 lbs.)**
- 2 **Tbsp. steak seasoning**
- ½ **cup water**
- 1 **half-pint jar pomegranate jelly or 1 cup red currant jelly**
- 3 **Tbsp. minced chipotle peppers in adobo sauce**
- 10 **kaiser rolls, split**
  Deli coleslaw, optional

1. Cut roast in half. Place meat in a 5-qt. slow cooker; sprinkle with steak seasoning. Add water. Cover and cook on low for 8-10 hours or until meat is tender.

2. In a small saucepan, combine jelly and peppers. Cook over medium heat for 5 minutes or until heated through. Remove meat from slow cooker; discard cooking liquid. Shred pork with 2 forks. Return to the slow cooker; top with jelly mixture. Cover and cook on low for 30 minutes or until heated through. Spoon about ⅔ cup meat onto each roll. If desired, top with coleslaw.

1 sandwich: 616 cal., 28g fat (10g sat. fat), 117mg chol., 839mg sod., 51g carb. (21g sugars, 1g fiber), 37g pro.

EGG DROP SOUP

We often start our stir-fry meals with this fast egg drop soup — it cooks in just minutes flat. There are many versions of the recipe, but we like the easy addition of cornstarch to thicken the soup and give it a rich, golden color. I got the recipe from my grandma's old cookbook.

—Amy Beth Corlew-Sherlock, Lapeer, MI

- -

Takes: 15 min.
Makes: 4 servings

3 cups chicken broth
1 Tbsp. cornstarch
2 Tbsp. cold water
1 large egg, lightly beaten
1 green onion, sliced

1. In a large saucepan, bring broth to a boil over medium heat. Combine cornstarch and water until smooth; gradually stir into broth. Bring to a boil; cook and stir for 2 minutes or until thickened.
2. Reduce heat. Drizzle beaten egg into hot broth, stirring constantly. Remove from the heat; stir in onion.

¾ cup: 39 cal., 2g fat (0 sat. fat), 53mg chol., 714mg sod., 3g carb. (1g sugars, 0 fiber), 3g pro.

★ ★ ★ ★ ★ **READER REVIEW**
"My husband and daughter were both convinced I bought this from our favorite Chinese restaurant."
—DRAGONSLAYERROSEBUD, TASTEOFHOME.COM

EGG DROP SOUP

SWEET & SPICY PEANUT BUTTER-BACON SANDWICHES

6 cups reduced-sodium chicken broth
½ tsp. salt
⅛ tsp. pepper
½ pkg. (8 oz.) uncooked fine egg noodles, cooked
Chopped fresh parsley, optional

1. Select saute setting on a 3- or 6-qt. electric pressure cooker and adjust for medium heat; add oil. Brown the chicken thighs. Press cancel. Add carrots, celery and broth to pressure cooker. Lock lid; close the pressure-release valve. Adjust to pressure-cook on high for 10 minutes. Allow the pressure to release naturally for 10 minutes, then quick-release any remaining pressure.

2. Stir in salt and pepper. Evenly divide noodles among 4 serving bowls. Add 1 chicken thigh to each bowl and top with broth. If desired, sprinkle with parsley.

2 cups soup with 1 chicken thigh: 389 cal., 29g fat (5g sat. fat), 112mg chol., 1262mg sod., 25g carb. (4g sugars, 2g fiber), 31g pro.

SWEET & SPICY PEANUT BUTTER-BACON SANDWICHES

I often craved peanut butter and bacon toast while pregnant. I tried a friend's peanut butter with chile pepper in it and loved it. The little zip truly made the sandwich better.

—Carolyn Eskew, Dayton, OH

- -

Takes: 10 min. • **Makes:** 2 servings

¼ cup peanut butter
4 slices cinnamon-raisin bread
⅛ tsp. cayenne pepper
4 crisp cooked bacon strips
2 tsp. honey

Spread peanut butter on 2 bread slices; sprinkle with cayenne. Top with bacon and drizzle with honey. Top with remaining bread.

1 sandwich: 461 cal., 26g fat (6g sat. fat), 23mg chol., 664mg sod., 43g carb. (15g sugars, 6g fiber), 21g pro.

GRANDMA'S PRESSURE-COOKER CHICKEN NOODLE SOUP

I've made this soup weekly since I modified my grandma's recipe for the pressure cooker. Chicken soup, especially this one, is quick to make and budget-friendly for any large family.

—Tammy Stanko, Greensburg, PA

- -

Prep: 10 min.
Cook: 25 min. + releasing
Makes: 4 servings

2 tsp. olive oil
4 bone-in chicken thighs
2 medium carrots, sliced
1½ celery ribs, sliced

GRANDMA'S PRESSURE-COOKER
CHICKEN NOODLE SOUP

BURGER AMERICANA

*Go on a burger road trip in your
own backyard. Grill the patties
and load them sky-high with
your favorite toppings. For
instance, peanut butter and
bacon make them southern
style; coleslaw and tomatoes,
a northern version.*

—Susan Mahaney, New Hartford, NY

- -

Takes: 25 min. • **Makes:** 4 servings

½ **cup seasoned bread crumbs**
1 **large egg, lightly beaten**
½ **tsp. salt**
½ **tsp. pepper**
1 **lb. ground beef**
1 **Tbsp. olive oil**
4 **sesame seed hamburger
   buns, split**
   Toppings of your choice

1. In a large bowl, combine bread
crumbs, egg, salt and pepper. Add
beef; mix lightly but thoroughly.
Shape into four ½-in.-thick patties.
Press a shallow indentation in the
center of each patty with your
thumb. Brush both sides of patties
with oil.

2. Grill the burgers, covered, over
medium heat or broil 4 in. from heat
4-5 minutes on each side or until a
thermometer reads 160°. Serve on
buns with toppings.

1 burger: 429 cal., 20g fat (6g sat.
fat), 123mg chol., 796mg sod., 32g
carb. (3g sugars, 1g fiber), 28g pro.

ASIAN RAMEN SHRIMP SOUP

A package of store-bought ramen noodles will speed up assembly of this colorful broth flavored with carrots and small shrimp. My mother passed the recipe on to me, It's delicious and so quick to make on busy nights.
—Donna Hellinger, Lorain, OH

- -

Takes: 15 min. • **Makes:** 4 servings

- 3½ cups water
- 1 pkg. (3 oz.) soy sauce ramen noodles
- 1 cup cooked small shrimp, peeled and deveined
- ½ cup chopped green onions
- 1 medium carrot, julienned
- 2 Tbsp. soy sauce

1. In a large saucepan, bring water to a boil. Set aside seasoning packet from noodles. Add the noodles to the boiling water; cook and stir for 3 minutes.
2. Add the shrimp, onions, carrot, soy sauce and contents of seasoning packet. Cook until heated through, 3-4 minutes longer.
1 cup: 148 cal., 4g fat (2g sat. fat), 83mg chol., 857mg sod., 17g carb. (2g sugars, 1g fiber), 12g pro.
Diabetic exchanges: 1 starch, 1 lean meat.

ASIAN RAMEN SHRIMP SOUP

BACON-WRAPPED HOT DOGS

Here's a satisfying meal-in-a-bun I take to tailgate parties, picnics, cookouts and more. I wrap the stuffed hot dogs in foil, then in paper, to transport them.
—Peter Halferty, Corpus Christi, TX

- -

Prep: 25 min. • **Grill:** 10 min.
Makes: 8 servings

- 12 bacon strips
- 8 cheese beef hot dogs
- 8 bakery hot dog buns, split and toasted
- ¼ cup chopped red onion
- 2 cups sauerkraut, rinsed and well drained
   Optional condiments: Mayonnaise, ketchup or Dijon mustard

1. In a large skillet, cook bacon over medium heat until partially cooked but not crisp. Drain on paper towels; cool slightly. Wrap 1½ bacon strips around each hot dog, securing with the toothpicks as needed (do not wrap tightly, or bacon may tear during grilling).
2. Grill, covered, over medium heat or broil 4 in. from heat 6-8 minutes or until bacon is crisp and hot dogs are heated through, turning them frequently. Discard the toothpicks. Serve hot dogs in buns with onion and sauerkraut; top with condiments of your choice.
1 stuffed hot dog: 360 cal., 22g fat (9g sat. fat), 47mg chol., 1119mg sod., 25g carb. (4g sugars, 2g fiber), 16g pro.

**CREAMY
CHICKEN SOUP**

CREAMY CHICKEN SOUP

Kids won't think twice about eating their vegetables after tasting this cheesy soup.
—LaVonne Lundgren, Sioux City, IA

- -

Takes: 30 min.
Makes: 8 servings (2⅔ qt.)

- 4   cups shredded cooked chicken breast
- 3½ cups water
- 2   cans (10¾ oz. each) condensed cream of chicken soup, undiluted
- 1   pkg. (16 oz.) frozen mixed vegetables, thawed
- 1   can (14½ oz.) diced potatoes, drained
- 1   lb. Velveeta, cubed
     Minced chives, optional

In a Dutch oven, combine the first 5 ingredients. Bring to a boil. Reduce the heat; cover and simmer until the vegetables are tender, 8-10 minutes. Stir in cheese just until melted (do not boil). If desired, top with minced fresh chives.

1⅓ cups: 429 cal., 22g fat (11g sat. fat), 116mg chol., 1464mg sod., 23g carb. (6g sugars, 4g fiber), 33g pro.

★ ★ ★ ★ ★ **READER REVIEW**

"This was quick and easy. I used rotisserie chicken to speed it up even more."
—KATLAYDEE3, TASTEOFHOME.COM

EASY GRILLED
HAMBURGERS

EASY GRILLED HAMBURGERS

Grill these easy hamburgers and add your favorite toppings. Not into grilling? Make the patties on the stovetop, in the oven or even in the air fryer.

—James Schend, Pleasant Prairie, WI

- -

Prep: 20 min. • **Grill:** 15 min.
Makes: 4 servings

1⅓ lbs. ground beef
¾ tsp. salt
¼ tsp. pepper
4 hamburger buns, split
and toasted
Optional toppings: Lettuce
leaves, sliced tomato, sliced
onion, bacon and mayonnaise

Shape the ground beef into four ¾-in.-thick patties. Before grilling, sprinkle with salt and pepper. Grill burgers, covered, over medium heat until a thermometer reads 160°, 5-7 minutes on each side. Top bun bottoms with burgers. If desired, serve with lettuce, tomato, onion, bacon and mayonnaise.

1 burger: 265 cal., 13g fat (5g sat. fat), 62mg chol., 495mg sod., 15g carb. (2g sugars, 1g fiber), 21g pro.

Pan-Fried Burgers: In a skillet, heat 1 Tbsp. butter or oil over medium heat. Add the burgers; cook until a thermometer reads 160°, 6-8 minutes on each side.

Oven-Baked Burgers: Place patties on a lightly greased baking sheet. Bake at 350° until a thermometer reads 160°, 15-20 minutes, turning once.

Air-Fried Burgers: Place burgers in a single layer on tray in air-fryer basket. Air-fry at 350° until a thermometer reads 160°, 8-10 minutes, turning halfway through cooking.

TEST KITCHEN TIP
Because these burgers only call for a handful of ingredients, you can get creative with the toppings. Try fresh basil leaves, salsa, corn relish, sliced jalapenos or pizza sauce.

GUMBO IN A JIFFY

AIR-FRYER REUBEN CALZONES

GUMBO IN A JIFFY

This is such a yummy dish. My husband loves the kick that the sausage gives this quick gumbo, and it's such a cinch to assemble.
—Amy Flack, Homer City, PA

- -

Takes: 20 min.
Makes: 6 servings

- 1 pkg. (12 oz.) smoked sausage, sliced
- 1 can (14½ oz.) diced tomatoes with green peppers and onions, undrained
- 1 can (14½ oz.) chicken broth
- ½ cup water
- 1 cup uncooked instant rice
- 1 can (7 oz.) whole kernel corn, drained
   Sliced green onions, optional

In a large saucepan, cook sliced sausage until browned on both sides. Stir in the tomatoes, broth and water; bring to a boil. Stir in rice and corn; cover and remove from the heat. Let stand for 5 minutes. If desired, top with sliced green onions.
1 cup: 279 cal., 16g fat (7g sat. fat), 40mg chol., 1197mg sod., 22g carb. (6g sugars, 2g fiber), 11g pro.

AIR-FRYER REUBEN CALZONES

I love a Reuben sandwich, so I tried the fillings in a pizza pocket instead of on rye bread. This hand-held dinner is a big-time winner at our house.
—Nickie Frye, Evansville, IN

- -

Prep: 15 min. • **Cook:** 10 min./batch
Makes: 4 servings

- 1 tube (13.8 oz.) refrigerated pizza crust
- 4 slices Swiss cheese
- 1 cup sauerkraut, rinsed and well drained
- ½ lb. sliced cooked corned beef
   Thousand Island salad dressing

1. Preheat air fryer to 400°. On a lightly floured surface, unroll the pizza crust dough and pat into a 12-in. square. Cut into 4 squares. Layer 1 slice cheese and a fourth of the sauerkraut and corned beef diagonally over half of each square to within ½ in. of the edges. Fold 1 corner over filling to the opposite corner, forming a triangle; press edges with a fork to seal. Place 2 calzones in a single layer on a greased tray in the air-fryer basket.

2. Cook until golden brown, 8-12 minutes, flipping halfway through. Serve with salad dressing.
1 calzone: 430 cal., 17g fat (6g sat. fat), 66mg chol., 1471mg sod., 49g carb. (7g sugars, 2g fiber), 21g pro.

TEST KITCHEN TIP
At the *Taste of Home* Test Kitchen, we found that the cook times vary quite a bit between different brands of air fryers. As a result, we have given wider than normal ranges on cook times. Begin checking food at the first time listed and adjust as needed.

SIMPLY ELEGANT TOMATO SOUP

If you've only had tomato soup from a can, you're going to be blown away when you try a bowl of this. It's velvety, creamy and oh-so-good!

—Heidi Blanken, Sedro-Woolley, WA

- - - - - - - - - - - - - - - - - - - -

Prep: 25 min. • **Cook:** 20 min.
Makes: 4 servings

- 4 lbs. tomatoes (about 10 medium)
- 1 Tbsp. butter
- 3 Tbsp. minced chives, divided
- 1 tsp. salt
- ½ tsp. pepper
- 2 cups half-and-half cream

1. In a large saucepan, bring 8 cups of water to a boil. Using a slotted spoon, carefully place the tomatoes, 1 at a time, in the boiling water for 30-60 seconds. Remove each tomato and immediately plunge in ice water. Peel and quarter tomatoes; remove the seeds.

2. In another large saucepan, melt butter. Add the tomatoes, 2 Tbsp. chives, salt and pepper. Bring to a boil. Reduce heat; simmer, uncovered, for 6-7 minutes or until tender, stirring occasionally. Remove from the heat. Cool slightly.

3. In a blender, process soup until blended. Return to the pan. Stir in cream; heat through. Sprinkle each serving with remaining chives.

1 cup: 268 cal., 16g fat (10g sat. fat), 68mg chol., 693mg sod., 22g carb. (16g sugars, 6g fiber), 8g pro.

HAWAIIAN SAUSAGE SUBS

If you are looking for a different way to use kielbasa, the sweet and mildly spicy flavor of these sandwiches is a nice change.

—Judy Dames, Bridgeville, PA

- - - - - - - - - - - - - - - - - - - -

Prep: 15 min. • **Cook:** 3 hours
Makes: 12 sandwiches

- 3 lbs. smoked kielbasa or Polish sausage, cut into 3-in. pieces
- 2 bottles (12 oz. each) chili sauce
- 1 can (20 oz.) pineapple tidbits, undrained
- ¼ cup packed brown sugar
- 12 hoagie buns, split
  Thinly sliced green onions, optional

Place kielbasa in a 3-qt. slow cooker. Combine the chili sauce, pineapple and brown sugar; pour over kielbasa. Cover and cook on low until heated through, 3-4 hours. Serve on buns. If desired, top with green onions.

1 sandwich: 663 cal., 35g fat (12g sat. fat), 76mg chol., 2532mg sod., 64g carb. (27g sugars, 1g fiber), 23g pro.

TEST KITCHEN TIP
Wow the crowd at the next potluck or tailgate when you wrap these sausage subs individually in foil. Transport them in an insulated cooler so they'll stay warm.

HAWAIIAN SAUSAGE SUBS

HAM & CHEESE
POCKETS

HAM & CHEESE POCKETS

These unique sandwich pockets are filled with ingredients both kids and adults enjoy.

—Callie Myers, Rockport, TX

- -

Prep: 15 min. + rising • **Bake:** 15 min.
Makes: 10 servings

- 1 **loaf (1 lb.) frozen bread dough, thawed**
- 2½ **cups finely chopped fully cooked ham**
- 1 **cup shredded Swiss cheese**
- 1 **large egg yolk**
- 1 **Tbsp. water**

1. Let dough rise according to package directions. Punch down; divide into 10 pieces. On a lightly floured surface, roll each piece into a 5-in. circle.

2. Preheat oven to 375°. Place 1 circle on a greased baking sheet; top with about ¼ cup ham and 2 Tbsp. cheese to within ½ in. of edge. Press filling to flatten. Combine egg yolk and water; brush edges of dough. Fold the dough over the filling and pinch the edges to seal. Repeat with remaining dough and filling. Brush tops with the remaining egg yolk mixture.

3. Bake until pockets are golden brown, 15-20 minutes. Serve warm or cold.

1 pocket: 229 cal., 9g fat (3g sat. fat), 50mg chol., 729mg sod., 25g carb. (2g sugars, 1g fiber), 14g pro.

MAIN COURSES

MUFFIN-TIN LASAGNAS
P. 136

1

2

3

4

5

SAVOR HOME-STYLE FAVORITES, KID-FRIENDLY DINNERS,
HEALTHY SUPPERS AND EVEN DATE-NIGHT DAZZLERS.
ALL ARE READY IN A WINK!

APPLE, WHITE CHEDDAR & ARUGULA TARTS

CHEESY BLACK BEAN NACHOS

We're trying to go meatless once a week, and this dish helps make those meals fun, quick and super delicious. It's also a smart way to use up beans and canned tomatoes from your pantry.
—Cynthia Nelson, Saskatoon, SK

- -

Takes: 20 min. • **Makes:** 4 servings

1   can (15 oz.) black beans, rinsed and drained
1   can (14½ oz.) diced tomatoes, well drained
3   to 4 jalapeno peppers, seeded and sliced
4   cups multigrain tortilla chips
1   cup shredded cheddar cheese
    Optional toppings: Sour cream, chopped fresh cilantro and additional jalapeno slices

1. Preheat oven to 350°. Mix beans, tomatoes and jalapenos. Arrange tortilla chips in an even layer in a 15x10x1-in. pan. Top with the bean mixture and cheese.
2. Bake, uncovered, until the cheese is melted, 10-12 minutes. Serve immediately with toppings as desired.
Note: Wear disposable gloves when cutting hot peppers; the oils can burn skin. Avoid touching your face.
1 serving: 371 cal., 17g fat (6g sat. fat), 28mg chol., 672mg sod., 42g carb. (6g sugars, 7g fiber), 15g pro.

APPLE, WHITE CHEDDAR & ARUGULA TARTS

These tarts remind me of fall in Michigan, where I grew up. Add meat if you like or keep it light. I always like to garnish the tarts with fried prosciutto.
—Maria Davis, Hermosa Beach, CA

- -

Takes: 30 min. • **Makes:** 4 servings

1   sheet frozen puff pastry, thawed
1   cup shredded white cheddar cheese
2   medium apples, thinly sliced
2   Tbsp. olive oil
1   Tbsp. lemon juice
3   cups fresh arugula or baby spinach

1. Preheat oven to 400°. On a lightly floured surface, unfold puff pastry; roll into a 12-in. square. Cut the pastry into 4 squares; place on a parchment-lined baking sheet.
2. Sprinkle half of each square with cheese to within ¼ in. of edges; top with apples. Fold pastry over filling. Press edges with a fork to seal. Bake until golden brown, 16-18 minutes.
3. In a bowl, whisk oil and lemon juice until blended; add arugula and toss to coat. Serve with tarts.
1 tart: 518 cal., 33g fat (10g sat. fat), 29mg chol., 389mg sod., 46g carb. (8g sugars, 7g fiber), 12g pro.

**CHEESY BLACK
BEAN NACHOS**

BREADED PORK TENDERLOIN

BREADED PORK TENDERLOIN

Meat is a hard sell with my teenage daughter unless I make it look like a restaurant dish. Drizzle ranch dressing or barbecue sauce on top and it's a home run.

—Donna Carney, New Lexington, OH

- -

Takes: 30 min. • **Makes:** 4 servings

1	**pork tenderloin (1 lb.)**
⅓	**cup all-purpose flour**
⅓	**cup cornbread/muffin mix**
½	**tsp. salt**
¼	**tsp. pepper**
1	**large egg, beaten**
4	**Tbsp. canola oil** **Ranch or barbecue sauce,** **optional**

1. Cut pork crosswise into ½-in. slices. In a shallow bowl, mix flour, cornbread mix, salt and pepper. Place egg in a separate shallow bowl. Dip pork in the egg, then in flour mixture, patting to help the coating adhere.

2. In a large skillet, heat 2 Tbsp. oil over medium heat. Add half of the pork; cook until a thermometer reads 145°, 3-4 minutes on each side. Drain on paper towels. Wipe skillet clean; repeat with remaining oil and pork. If desired, serve with sauce.

3 oz. cooked pork: 338 cal., 20g fat (3g sat. fat), 110mg chol., 327mg sod., 12g carb. (2g sugars, 1g fiber), 26g pro.

★ ★ ★ ★ ★ **READER REVIEW**

"Used boneless center-cut pork chops instead of tenderloin. This is definitely a new and unique way to bread pork chops for me. Generally I just use regular bread crumbs. These came out great. I will be making them again."

—CYNTHIAJOSCHER, TASTEOFHOME.COM

CHICKEN ENCHILADA BAKE

Good thing the recipe makes a lot, because your family won't want to stop eating this cheesy southwestern casserole. The green enchilada sauce brightens it right up.

—Melanie Burns, Pueblo West, CO

- -

Prep: 20 min.
Bake: 50 min. + standing
Makes: 10 servings

- 4½ cups shredded rotisserie chicken
- 1 can (28 oz.) green enchilada sauce
- 1¼ cups sour cream
- 9 corn tortillas (6 in.), cut into 1½-in. pieces
- 4 cups shredded Monterey Jack cheese
  Fresh minced parsley, optional

1. Preheat oven to 375°. In a greased 13x9-in. baking dish, layer half of each of the following: chicken, enchilada sauce, sour cream, tortillas and cheese. Repeat layers.
2. Bake, covered, for 40 minutes. Uncover; bake until bubbly, about 10 minutes longer. Let stand for 15 minutes before serving. If desired, sprinkle with parsley.

Freeze option: Cover and freeze unbaked casserole. To use, partially thaw in refrigerator overnight. Remove from refrigerator 30 minutes before baking. Preheat oven to 375°. Bake casserole as directed, increasing time as necessary to heat through and for a thermometer inserted in center to read 165° If desired, sprinkle with parsley.

1 cup: 428 cal., 27g fat (14g sat. fat), 103mg chol., 709mg sod., 16g carb. (3g sugars, 1g fiber), 32g pro.

POLISH KRAUT WITH APPLES

The combination of apples, sauerkraut and smoked sausage gives this hearty dinner an old-world flavor. I enjoy making this because it's so easy to prepare.

—Caren Markee, Cary, IL

- -

Prep: 10 min. • **Cook:** 3 hours
Makes: 2 servings

- 1 cup sauerkraut, rinsed and well drained
- ½ lb. smoked Polish sausage or kielbasa, cut up
- 1 large tart apple, peeled and cut into eighths
- ¼ cup packed brown sugar
- ¼ tsp. caraway seeds, optional
  Dash pepper
- ⅓ cup apple juice

1. Place half the sauerkraut in an ungreased 1½-qt. slow cooker. Top with sausage, apples, brown sugar, caraway seeds if desired, and pepper. Top with remaining sauerkraut. Pour apple juice over all.
2. Cover and cook on low 3-4 hours or until apples are tender.

1 cup: 522 cal., 30g fat (10g sat. fat), 81mg chol., 1440mg sod., 49g carb. (41g sugars, 3g fiber), 15g pro.

CHICKEN ENCHILADA BAKE

HONEY WALLEYE

HONEY WALLEYE

Our state is known as the Land of 10,000 Lakes, so fishing is a favorite recreational activity here. This recipe is a quick way to prepare all the fresh walleye hooked by the anglers in our family.
—Kitty McCue, St. Louis Park, MN

- -

Takes: 20 min. • **Makes:** 6 servings

1   **large egg**
2   **tsp. honey**
2   **cups crushed Ritz crackers (about 45 to 50)**
½   **tsp. salt**
1½   **lbs. walleye fillets**
⅓   **to ½ cup canola oil**
     Optional: Minced fresh parsley and lemon wedges

1. In a shallow bowl, beat egg; add honey. In a shallow dish, combine crackers and salt. Dip fish in egg mixture, then in cracker mixture; turn until coated.

2. In a cast-iron or other heavy skillet, cook fillets in oil over medium heat until golden and fish flakes easily with a fork, 3-5 minutes on each side. If desired, top with parsley and serve with lemon wedges.

3 oz. cooked fish: 389 cal., 22g fat (3g sat. fat), 133mg chol., 514mg sod., 23g carb. (5g sugars, 1g fiber), 25g pro.

GRILLED STEAK BRUSCHETTA SALAD FOR 2

GRILLED STEAK BRUSCHETTA SALAD FOR 2

Fire up the grill for this tasty salad. The meat will be done in a snap, leaving you more time to enjoy the summer evening.
—Devon Delaney, Westport, CT

- -

Takes: 25 min. • **Makes:** 2 servings

½ **lb. beef tenderloin steaks**
  (**1 in. thick**)
¼ **tsp. salt**
⅛ **tsp. pepper**

2 **slices Italian bread**
  (**½ in. thick**)
1 **cup fresh arugula**
  or fresh baby spinach
⅓ **cup jarred or prepared**
  bruschetta topping
⅓ **cup blue cheese salad**
  dressing

1. Sprinkle steaks with salt and pepper. Grill, covered, over medium heat until meat reaches desired doneness (for medium-rare, a thermometer should read 135°; medium, 140°; medium-well, 145°), 6-8 minutes on each side. Let stand for 5 minutes.

2. Grill bread, covered, until toasted, 1-2 minutes on each side; place on salad plates.

3. Thinly slice steak; arrange over toast. Top with arugula and the bruschetta topping. Drizzle with salad dressing.

Note: Look for bruschetta topping in the pasta aisle or your grocer's deli case.

1 serving: 460 cal., 31g fat (7g sat. fat), 57mg chol., 1183mg sod., 17g carb. (3g sugars, 1g fiber), 28g pro.

LEMON-GARLIC
SALMON STEAKS

LEMON-GARLIC SALMON STEAKS

I always enjoy making this easy recipe for my husband, Jim. He absolutely loves salmon and garlic, and they go together so well in this recipe.

—Mary Lynn Baronett, Waynesburg, PA

- -

Prep: 10 min. • **Bake:** 25 min.
Makes: 6 servings

- 6 to 8 garlic cloves, minced
- 4 Tbsp. olive oil, divided
- 6 salmon steaks (6 oz. each)
- ⅔ cup lemon juice
- ¼ cup minced fresh parsley
  Salt and pepper to taste

1. Preheat oven to 350°. In a small skillet, saute garlic in 1 Tbsp. oil for 1 minute.

2. Arrange salmon steaks in a greased 13x9-in. baking dish. Combine lemon juice, parsley, salt, pepper and remaining oil; pour over salmon. Top with garlic mixture.

3. Bake, uncovered, 25-30 minutes or until fish flakes easily with a fork.

1 salmon steak: 403 cal., 27g fat (5g sat. fat), 100mg chol., 103mg sod., 3g carb. (1g sugars, 0 fiber), 34g pro.

Tarragon Salmon Steaks: Omit garlic and olive oil. Stir 3 Tbsp. melted butter and 3 Tbsp. minced fresh tarragon into the lemon juice mixture. Proceed as directed.

BIG KAHUNA PIZZA

BIG KAHUNA PIZZA

A prebaked pizza crust and refrigerated barbecued pork make this tasty supper idea super fast and super easy. Cut into bite-sized pieces, it can double as a great last-minute appetizer, too!

—Joni Hilton, Rocklin, CA

- -

Takes: 30 min. • **Makes:** 8 servings

- 1 prebaked 12-in. pizza crust
- 1 carton (16 oz.) refrigerated fully cooked barbecued shredded pork
- 1 can (20 oz.) pineapple chunks, drained
- ⅓ cup chopped red onion
- 2 cups shredded part-skim mozzarella cheese

1. Place pizza crust on an ungreased 12-in. pizza pan. Spread shredded pork over crust; top with pineapple and onion. Sprinkle with cheese.

2. Bake at 350° for 20-25 minutes or until cheese is melted.

1 piece: 343 cal., 10g fat (4g sat. fat), 33mg chol., 856mg sod., 45g carb. (20g sugars, 2g fiber), 19g pro.

PINEAPPLE-DIJON PORK CHOPS

I like to dress up pork chops with pineapple, peach or apricot preserves. Whenever I do, I always serve mashed sweet potatoes on the side. They make a perfect pair.

—Jane Whittaker, Pensacola, FL

- -

Takes: 25 min. • **Makes:** 4 servings

4	boneless pork loin chops (6 oz. each)
½	tsp. seasoned salt
1	Tbsp. canola oil
¾	cup pineapple preserves
¼	cup chardonnay or chicken broth
3	Tbsp. Dijon mustard

1. Sprinkle pork chops with seasoned salt. In a large skillet, heat oil over medium-high heat. Brown pork chops on both sides.

2. In a small bowl, mix preserves, chardonnay and mustard; add to pan. Reduce heat; simmer, covered, 5-7 minutes or until a thermometer inserted in pork reads 145°. Let stand 5 minutes before serving.

1 pork chop with ¼ cup sauce: 428 cal., 13g fat (4g sat. fat), 82mg chol., 508mg sod., 39g carb. (36g sugars, 0 fiber), 33g pro.

MUFFIN-TIN LASAGNAS

This is a super fun way to serve lasagna and a great way to surprise everyone at the table. Easy and quick, these little cups can be made with whatever ingredients your family likes best.

—Sally Kilkenny, Granger, IA

- -

Takes: 30 min. • **Makes:** 1 dozen

1	large egg, lightly beaten
1	carton (15 oz.) part-skim ricotta cheese
2	cups shredded Italian cheese blend, divided
1	Tbsp. olive oil
24	wonton wrappers
1	jar (24 oz.) garden-style pasta sauce
	Minced fresh parsley, optional

1. Preheat oven to 375°. In a bowl, mix egg, ricotta cheese and 1¼ cups Italian cheese blend.

2. Generously grease 12 muffin cups with oil; line each with a wonton wrapper. Fill each with 1 Tbsp. ricotta mixture and 1½ Tbsp. pasta sauce. Top each with a second wrapper, rotating corners and pressing down centers. Repeat ricotta and sauce layers. Sprinkle with remaining cheese blend.

3. Bake until cheese is melted, 20-25 minutes. If desired, sprinkle with parsley.

2 mini lasagnas: 414 cal., 19g fat (9g sat. fat), 83mg chol., 970mg sod., 36g carb. (8g sugars, 2g fiber), 22g pro.

MUFFIN-TIN LASAGNAS

AIR-FRYER GARLIC-BUTTER STEAK

AIR-FRYER GARLIC-BUTTER STEAK

This quick and easy entree is definitely restaurant quality. Get ready for it to become a staple at your house!
—Lily Julow, Lawrenceville, GA

- -

Takes: 20 min. • **Makes:** 2 servings

- 1 **beef flat iron steak or boneless top sirloin steak (¾ lb.)**
- ⅛ **tsp. salt**
- ⅛ **tsp. pepper**
- 1 **Tbsp. butter, softened**
- 1 **tsp. minced fresh parsley**
- ½ **tsp. minced garlic**
- ¼ **tsp. reduced-sodium soy sauce**

1. Preheat air fryer to 400°. Sprinkle steak with salt and pepper. Place steak on tray in air-fryer basket. Cook until meat reaches desired doneness (for medium-rare, a thermometer should read 135°; medium, 140°; medium-well, 145°), 8-10 minutes, turning halfway through cooking.

2. Meanwhile, combine butter, parsley, garlic and soy sauce. Serve with steak.

4 oz. cooked beef with 2 tsp. garlic butter: 353 cal., 24g fat (11g sat. fat), 125mg chol., 322mg sod., 0 carb. (0 sugars, 0 fiber), 33g pro.

TEST KITCHEN TIP
If you don't have an air fryer, you can make this recipe on the stovetop.

**AIR-FRYER
ALMOND CHICKEN**

AIR-FRYER
ALMOND CHICKEN

*My husband bought an air fryer
after seeing it on television. We
have used it at least twice a week
and love how delicious the food
has been. The chicken recipes
we have tried are especially good
because of how moist the meat
remains. We started a low-carb
diet and did not want to use
bread crumbs, so we tried
making this dish with almonds.
It is a favorite now.*

—Pamela Shank, Parkersburg, WV

- -

Takes: 30 min. • **Makes:** 2 servings

1   **large egg**
¼   **cup buttermilk**
1   **tsp. garlic salt**
½   **tsp. pepper**
1   **cup slivered almonds,
      finely chopped**
2   **boneless skinless chicken
      breast halves (6 oz. each)
      Optional: Ranch salad
      dressing, barbecue sauce
      and honey mustard**

1. Preheat air fryer to 350°. In a
shallow bowl, whisk egg, buttermilk,
garlic salt and pepper. Place almonds
in another shallow bowl. Dip chicken
into egg mixture, then into almonds,
patting to help coating adhere.

2. Place chicken in a single layer on
greased tray in air-fryer basket; spritz
with cooking spray. Cook until a
thermometer inserted in chicken
reads at least 165°, 15-18 minutes. If
desired, serve with ranch dressing,
barbecue sauce or mustard.

1 chicken breast half: 353 cal., 18g
fat (2g sat. fat), 123mg chol., 230mg
sod., 6g carb. (2g sugars, 3g fiber),
41g pro.

BACON CHEESEBURGER PASTA

I make foods that are kid friendly but also easy to reheat since my husband works long hours and often eats later than our children. If you like, you can use reduced-fat cheese and ground turkey for a lighter version.

—Melissa Stevens, Elk River, MN

Takes: 30 min. • **Makes:** 6 servings

- 8   oz. uncooked penne pasta
- 1   lb. ground beef
- 6   bacon strips, diced
- 1   can (10¾ oz.) condensed tomato soup, undiluted
- ½   cup water
- 1   cup shredded cheddar cheese
     Optional: Barbecue sauce and prepared mustard

1. Cook pasta according to the package directions. Meanwhile, in a large skillet, cook beef over medium heat until no longer pink; drain and set aside.

2. In the same skillet, cook bacon until crisp; remove with a slotted spoon to paper towels to drain. Discard drippings. Drain pasta; add to the skillet. Stir in the soup, water, beef and bacon; heat through.

3. Remove from the heat and sprinkle with cheese. Cover and let stand for 2-3 minutes or until the cheese is melted. Serve with barbecue sauce and mustard if desired.

1 serving: 389 cal., 16g fat (8g sat. fat), 62mg chol., 565mg sod., 36g carb. (5g sugars, 2g fiber), 25g pro.

BACON CHEESEBURGER PASTA

PRESSURE-COOKER SWISS STEAK

AIR-FRYER CHICKEN THIGHS

This air-fryer chicken thighs recipe creates meat that is crispy on the outside but super juicy on the inside. The paprika and garlic seasoning blend comes through beautifully.

—*Taste of Home* Test Kitchen

- -

Takes: 20 min. • **Makes:** 4 servings

  4 **bone-in chicken thighs (about 1½ lbs.)**
  1 **Tbsp. olive oil**
  ¾ **tsp. salt**
  ½ **tsp. paprika**
  ¼ **tsp. garlic powder**
  ¼ **tsp. pepper**

Preheat air fryer to 375°. Brush chicken with oil. Combine remaining ingredients; sprinkle over chicken. Place chicken, skin side up, in a single layer on tray in air-fryer basket. Cook until a thermometer inserted in chicken thigh reads 170°-175°, 15-17 minutes.

1 chicken thigh: 255 cal., 18g fat (4g sat. fat), 81mg chol., 511mg sod., 0 carb. (0 sugars, 0 fiber), 23g pro.

PRESSURE-COOKER SWISS STEAK

Swiss steak has a been a standby for family cooks for decades, and this no-fuss way to cook it promises to keep the entree popular for years to come. Best of all, it's low in calories and fat.

—Sarah Burks, Wathena, KS

- -

Prep: 10 min. • **Cook:** 20 min. + releasing • **Makes:** 6 servings

  1½ **lbs. beef round steak, cut into 6 pieces**
  ½ **tsp. salt**
  ¼ **tsp. pepper**
  1 **medium onion, cut into ¼-in. slices**
  1 **celery rib, cut into ½-in. slices**
  2 **cans (8 oz. each) tomato sauce**

Sprinkle steak with salt and pepper. Place onion in a 6-qt. electric pressure cooker. Top with celery, tomato sauce and steak. Lock lid; close pressure-release valve. Adjust to pressure-cook on high for 20 minutes. Let pressure release naturally for 5 minutes. then quick-release any remaining pressure. A thermometer inserted in steak should read at least 145°.

1 serving: 167 cal., 4g fat (1g sat. fat), 63mg chol., 581mg sod., 6g carb. (2g sugars, 2g fiber), 27g pro.
Diabetic exchanges: 3 lean meat, 1 vegetable.

**AIR-FRYER
CHICKEN THIGHS**

GRILLED MAPLE PORK CHOPS

Pork chops on the grill are hard to beat. The marinade is simple, and so good.

—Nicholas King, Duluth, MN

- -

Prep: 5 min. + marinating
Grill: 15 min. • **Makes:** 4 servings

- 6 Tbsp. maple syrup
- 6 Tbsp. balsamic vinegar
- ¾ tsp. salt
- ¾ tsp. coarsely ground pepper

- 4 boneless pork loin chops
(1½ in. thick and 12 oz. each)

1. In a small bowl, whisk syrup, vinegar, salt and pepper until blended. Pour ½ cup marinade into a shallow bowl. Add the pork chops; turn to coat. Cover and refrigerate 1 hour. Reserve remaining marinade for basting.

2. Drain pork chops, discarding marinade. On an oiled grill, cook pork chops, covered, over medium heat or broil 4 in. from heat until a thermometer reads 145°, 13-17 minutes, turning occasionally and basting with reserved marinade during the last 5 minutes. Let stand 5 minutes before serving.

1 pork chop: 509 cal., 19g fat (7g sat. fat), 164mg chol., 339mg sod., 15g carb. (14g sugars, 0 fiber), 65g pro.

POLENTA CHILI CASSEROLE

This delicious vegetarian bake combines spicy chili, mixed veggies and homemade polenta. It's so hearty that no one seems to miss the meat.
—Dan Kelmenson, West Bloomfield, MI

- -

Prep: 20 min.
Bake: 35 min. + standing
Makes: 8 servings

- 4 cups water
- ½ tsp. salt
- 1¼ cups yellow cornmeal
- 2 cups shredded cheddar cheese, divided
- 3 cans (15 oz. each) vegetarian chili with beans
- 1 pkg. (16 oz.) frozen mixed vegetables, thawed and well drained

1. Preheat oven to 350°. In a large heavy saucepan, bring water and salt to a boil. Reduce heat to a gentle boil; slowly whisk in cornmeal. Cook and stir with a wooden spoon until polenta is thickened and pulls away cleanly from the sides of pan, 15-20 minutes.

2. Remove from heat. Stir in ¼ cup cheddar cheese until melted.

3. Spread into a 13x9-in. baking dish coated with cooking spray. Bake, uncovered, 20 minutes. Meanwhile, heat chili according to package directions.

4. Spread vegetables over polenta; top with chili. Sprinkle with remaining cheese. Bake until cheese is melted, 12-15 minutes longer. Let stand 10 minutes before serving.

1 piece: 297 cal., 7g fat (4g sat. fat), 20mg chol., 556mg sod., 43g carb. (7g sugars, 12g fiber), 19g pro.

RYE BREAD-TOPPED REUBEN CASSEROLE

I always get compliments when I take this wonderful casserole to a potluck dinner.
—Nita White, Cedar Springs, MI

- -

Takes: 30 min. • **Makes:** 4 servings

- 1 can (14 oz.) sauerkraut, rinsed and well drained
- 1 cup Thousand Island salad dressing
- 1 lb. thinly sliced deli corned beef, cut into strips
- 2 cups shredded Swiss cheese
- 4 to 6 slices rye bread, buttered

1. In a large bowl, combine drained sauerkraut and salad dressing; spread into a greased 13x9-in. baking dish. Top with the corned beef and Swiss cheese.

2. Place bread, buttered side up, over top. Bake, uncovered, at 375° for 25-30 minutes or until heated through and bubbly.

1 cup: 705 cal., 44g fat (16g sat. fat), 143mg chol., 3149mg sod., 33g carb. (13g sugars, 5g fiber), 41g pro.

★ ★ ★ ★ ★ **READER REVIEW**

"Because of a family divide, I make half of the casserole with Thousand Island and half with Russian dressing, the REAL dressing for Reubens!"
—REBELWITHOUTACLUE, TASTEOFHOME.COM

POLENTA CHILI CASSEROLE

EASY CHICKEN STRIPS

I came up with these crispy strips one night when I was looking for a fast new way to serve chicken. They make delightful appetizers, too, especially when I serve them with barbecue or sweet-and-sour sauce for dunking.
—Crystal Sheckles-Gibson, Bee Spring, KY

- -

Takes: 30 min. • **Makes:** 6 servings

¼ cup all-purpose flour
¾ tsp. seasoned salt
1¼ cups crushed cornflakes
⅓ cup butter, melted
1½ lbs. boneless skinless chicken breasts, cut into 1-in. strips

1. Preheat oven to 400°. In a shallow bowl, combine flour and seasoned salt. Place cornflakes and butter in separate shallow bowls. Coat chicken with flour mixture, then dip in butter and coat with cornflakes.

2. Transfer chicken strips to an ungreased baking sheet. Bake until chicken is golden brown and juices run clear, 15-20 minutes.

3 oz. cooked chicken: 283 cal., 12g fat (7g sat. fat), 87mg chol., 438mg sod., 18g carb. (2g sugars, 0 fiber), 25g pro.

EASY CHICKEN STRIPS

BBQ MEAT LOAF MINIS

BBQ MEAT LOAF MINIS

Kids can have fun helping to prepare these mini meat loaves in muffin cups. If we're in the mood for extra spice, we add 2 teaspoons of chili powder and 1 cup of salsa.

—Linda Call, Falun, KS

- -

Takes: 30 min. • **Makes:** 6 servings

1 **pkg. (6 oz.) stuffing mix**
1 **cup water**
2 **Tbsp. hickory smoke-flavored barbecue sauce**
1 **lb. ground beef**
1 **cup shredded cheddar cheese**
  Additional hickory smoke-flavored barbecue sauce, optional

1. Preheat oven to 375°. In a large bowl, combine stuffing mix, water and 2 Tbsp. barbecue sauce. Add beef; mix lightly but thoroughly. Press ⅓ cup mixture into each of 12 ungreased muffin cups.

2. Bake meat loaves, uncovered, until a thermometer reads 160°, 18-22 minutes. Sprinkle tops with cheese; bake until cheese is melted, 2-4 minutes longer. If desired, serve with additional barbecue sauce.

Freeze option: Securely wrap and freeze cooled meat loaf in foil. To use, partially thaw in refrigerator overnight. Place meat loaves on a greased shallow baking pan. Bake in a preheated 350° oven until heated through. Top with cheese as directed.

2 mini meat loaves: 330 cal., 17g fat (7g sat. fat), 67mg chol., 668mg sod., 21g carb. (4g sugars, 1g fiber), 21g pro.

EASY CHICKEN PESTO STUFFED PEPPERS

EASY CHICKEN PESTO STUFFED PEPPERS

On busy weeknights, I don't want to spend more than 30 minutes preparing dinner, nor do I want to wash a towering pile of dishes. This recipe delivers without having to sacrifice flavor!
—Olivia Cruz, Greenville, SC

- -

Takes: 25 min. • **Makes:** 4 servings

- 4 medium sweet yellow or orange peppers
- 1½ cups shredded rotisserie chicken
- 1½ cups cooked brown rice
- 1 cup prepared pesto
- ½ cup shredded Havarti cheese
  Fresh basil leaves, optional

1. Cut peppers lengthwise in half; remove stems and seeds. Place peppers on a baking sheet, skin side up. Broil 4 in. from heat until skins blister, about 5 minutes. Reduce oven temperature to 350°.

2. Meanwhile, in a large bowl, combine chicken, rice and pesto. When cool enough to handle, fill peppers with chicken mixture; return to baking sheet. Bake until heated through, about 5 minutes. Sprinkle with cheese; bake until cheese is melted, 3-5 minutes. If desired, sprinkle with basil.

2 stuffed pepper halves: 521 cal., 31g fat (7g sat. fat), 62mg chol., 865mg sod., 33g carb. (7g sugars, 5g fiber), 25g pro.

CRUMB-COATED RED SNAPPER

CRUMB-COATED RED SNAPPER

I reel in compliments when I serve this moist, crispy red snapper recipe. Heart-healthy omega-3 oils are an added bonus with this simple but delicious entree that's ready in minutes. It's one of the best red snapper recipes I've found.
—Charlotte Elliott, Neenah, WI

- -

Takes: 30 min. • **Makes:** 4 servings

- ½ cup dry bread crumbs
- 2 Tbsp. grated Parmesan cheese
- 1 tsp. lemon-pepper seasoning
- ¼ tsp. salt
- 4 red snapper fillets (6 oz. each)
- 2 Tbsp. olive oil

1. In a shallow bowl, combine the bread crumbs, cheese, lemon pepper and salt; add fillets, 1 at a time, and turn to coat.

2. In a heavy skillet over medium heat, cook fillets in oil, in batches, until fish just begins to flake easily with a fork, 4-5 minutes on each side.

1 fillet: 288 cal., 10g fat (2g sat. fat), 62mg chol., 498mg sod., 10g carb. (0 sugars, 0 fiber), 36g pro. **Diabetic exchanges:** 5 lean meat, 1½ fat, ½ starch.

SAUSAGE MANICOTTI

This classic Italian entree comes together in a snap, but tastes like it took hours. It's so tasty and easy to fix. My family always enjoys it.

—Carolyn Henderson, Maple Plain, MN

- -

Prep: 15 min. • **Bake:** 65 min.
Makes: 7 servings

- 1 **lb. uncooked bulk pork sausage**
- 2 **cups 4% cottage cheese**
- 1 **pkg. (8 oz.) manicotti shells**
- 1 **jar (24 oz.) marinara sauce**
- 1 **cup shredded part-skim mozzarella cheese**

1. In a large bowl, combine sausage and cottage cheese. Stuff into uncooked manicotti shells. Place in a greased 13x9-in. baking dish. Top with marinara sauce.

2. Cover and bake at 350° until a thermometer inserted into the center of a manicotti shell reads 160°, 55-60 minutes.

3. Uncover; sprinkle with mozzarella cheese. Bake until cheese is melted, 8-10 minutes longer. Let stand for 5 minutes before serving.

Freeze option: Transfer individual portions of cooled manicotti to freezer containers; freeze. To use, partially thaw in the refrigerator overnight. Transfer to a microwave-safe dish and microwave on high, stirring occasionally; add a little spaghetti sauce if necessary.

2 pieces: 489 cal., 24g fat (10g sat. fat), 59mg chol., 1232mg sod., 41g carb. (12g sugars, 3g fiber), 27g pro.

BAKED SWISS CHICKEN

Canned soup, white wine, Swiss cheese and crushed croutons dress up the chicken breasts in this elegant entree. Ideal for unexpected guests, it requires only a few ingredients. The creamy sauce is excellent with garlic mashed potatoes or rice.

—Beverly Roberge, Bristol, CT

- -

Prep: 5 min. • **Bake:** 35 min.
Makes: 6 servings

- 6 **boneless skinless chicken breast halves (6 oz. each)**
- 1 **can (10¾ oz.) condensed cream of chicken soup, undiluted**
- ½ **cup white wine or chicken broth**
- 6 **slices Swiss cheese**
- 1 **cup crushed seasoned croutons**

1. Preheat oven to 350°. Place chicken in a greased 13x9-in. baking dish. Combine soup and wine; pour over chicken. Top with cheese and sprinkle with croutons.

2. Bake, uncovered, until a thermometer inserted in chicken reads 165°, 35-40 minutes.

1 serving: 308 cal., 13g fat (7g sat. fat), 92mg chol., 614mg sod., 11g carb. (1g sugars, 1g fiber), 31g pro.

BAKED SWISS CHICKEN

MEATBALL
TORTELLINI

MEATBALL TORTELLINI

*I combined some favorite staples
from our freezer and pantry to
come up with an easy dish. It
uses just a few ingredients and
requires little preparation.*
—Tracie Bergeron, Chauvin, LA

- -

Prep: 10 min. • **Cook:** 3 hours
Makes: 6 servings

1   **pkg. frozen fully cooked
Italian meatballs (12 oz.),
thawed**

2   **cups uncooked dried
cheese tortellini**
2   **cans (10¾ oz. each)
condensed cream of
mushroom soup, undiluted**
2¼ **cups water**
1   **tsp. Creole seasoning**
1   **pkg. (16 oz.) frozen
California-blend vegetables,
thawed**

1. In a 3-qt. slow cooker, combine
meatballs and tortellini. In a large
bowl, whisk cream of mushroom
soup, water and Creole seasoning.

Pour over meatball mixture; stir well.
2. Cook, covered, on low 3-4 hours
or until tortellini are tender. Add
vegetables during last half-hour
of cooking.

Note: If you don't have Creole
seasoning in your cupboard, you can
make your own using ¼ tsp. each salt,
garlic powder and paprika; and a pinch
each of dried thyme, ground cumin
and cayenne pepper.

1 cup: 408 cal., 23g fat (10g sat. fat),
55mg chol., 1592mg sod., 35g carb.
(3g sugars, 6g fiber), 16g pro.

SAUSAGE & SAUERKRAUT

SAUSAGE & SAUERKRAUT

Three young children involved in different activities keep me running year-round. I created this for those extra-busy nights. It delivers flavor—and makes life a little easier, too.

—Mary Lyon, Spotsylvania, VA

- -

Takes: 30 min. • **Makes:** 4 servings

6 medium red potatoes, cubed
2 Tbsp. canola oil
1 small onion, halved and sliced
1 lb. smoked sausage, cut into ¼-in. pieces
1 pkg. (16 oz.) sauerkraut, rinsed and well drained
¼ tsp. pepper

In a large skillet, saute potatoes in oil until lightly browned, 5-6 minutes. Stir in sliced onion; saute until tender, 3-4 minutes. Add smoked sausage, sauerkraut and pepper. Cook, uncovered, over medium heat until heated through, 4-5 minutes, stirring occasionally.

1½ cups: 567 cal., 38g fat (14g sat. fat), 76mg chol., 2043mg sod., 36g carb. (7g sugars, 6g fiber), 20g pro.

GRILLED PEPPERED STEAKS

I once wanted a peppered steak for supper, so I tossed some spices together and came up with this recipe. My family thoroughly enjoyed it.
—Stephanie Moon, Boise, ID

- -

Takes: 25 min. • **Makes:** 4 servings

- 1½ to 2 tsp. coarsely ground pepper
- 1 tsp. onion salt
- 1 tsp. garlic salt
- ¼ tsp. paprika, optional
- 4 boneless beef top loin steaks (8 oz. each)

1. In a small bowl, combine the pepper, onion salt, garlic salt and, if desired, paprika. Rub onto both sides of steaks.

2. Grill, covered, over medium heat until meat reaches desired doneness (for medium-rare, a thermometer should read 135°; medium, 140°; medium-well, 145°), 8-10 minutes on each side.

Note: Top loin steak may be labeled as strip steak, Kansas City steak, New York strip steak, ambassador steak or boneless club steak in your region.

1 steak: 301 cal., 10g fat (4g sat. fat), 100mg chol., 1039mg sod., 1g carb. (0 sugars, 0 fiber), 48g pro.

GRILLED PEPPERED STEAKS

MEAT LOAF IN A MUG

MEAT LOAF IN A MUG

Here's a quick, delicious single serving of meat loaf. This smart take on a classic gives you the traditional flavor of meat loaf with hardly any cleanup and no leftovers!

—Ruby Matt, Garnavillo, IA

- -

Takes: 15 min. • **Makes:** 1 serving

2	Tbsp. 2% milk
1	Tbsp. ketchup
2	Tbsp. quick-cooking oats
1	tsp. onion soup mix
¼	lb. lean ground beef

1. In a small bowl, combine milk, ketchup, oats and soup mix. Crumble beef over mixture and mix well. Pat into a microwave-safe mug or custard cup coated with cooking spray.

2. Cover and microwave on high for 3 minutes or until meat is no longer pink and a thermometer reads 160°; drain. Let stand for 3 minutes. If desired, serve meat loaf with additional ketchup.

1 serving: 316 cal., 14g fat (5g sat. fat), 100mg chol., 471mg sod., 14g carb. (6g sugars, 1g fiber), 33g pro.

BEEF & RICE ENCHILADAS

With a toddler in the house, I look for foods that are a snap to make. Loaded with beef, cheese and a flavorful rice mix, these enchiladas come together without any fuss. But they're so good that guests think I spent hours in the kitchen.

—Jennifer Smith, Colona, IL

- -

Prep: 30 min. • **Bake:** 20 min.
Makes: 10 enchiladas

1	pkg. (6.8 oz.) Spanish rice and pasta mix
1	lb. ground beef
2	cans (10 oz. each) enchilada sauce, divided
10	flour tortillas (8 in.), warmed
1⅔	cups shredded cheddar cheese, divided

1. Prepare rice mix according to package directions. Meanwhile, in a large skillet, cook beef over medium heat until no longer pink; drain. Stir in Spanish rice and 1¼ cups enchilada sauce.

2. Spoon about ⅔ cup beef mixture down the center of each tortilla. Top each with 1 Tbsp. cheese; roll up.

3. Place in an ungreased 13x9-in. baking dish. Top with the remaining enchilada sauce and cheese. Bake, uncovered, at 350° until the cheese is melted, 20-25 minutes.

1 enchilada: 415 cal., 17g fat (8g sat. fat), 47mg chol., 1141mg sod., 46g carb. (3g sugars, 3g fiber), 20g pro.

BEEF & RICE
ENCHILADAS

SIZZLING ANCHO RIBEYES FOR TWO

SIZZLING ANCHO RIBEYES FOR TWO

We love the taste of chipotle peppers, which are smoked and dried jalapenos, on just about anything. This simple, delicious recipe proves that chipotle pairs perfectly with grilled steak.

—Angela Spengler, Niceville, FL

- -

Takes: 25 min. • **Makes:** 2 servings

¾ tsp. salt
¾ tsp. ground ancho chile
     pepper
⅛ tsp. pepper
2 beef ribeye steaks
     (¾ lb. each)
2 Tbsp. butter, softened
2 chipotle peppers in adobo
     sauce, minced, plus ¼ tsp.
     adobo sauce

1. In a small bowl, combine the salt, chile pepper and pepper; rub over the steaks.

2. In another small bowl, beat the butter, chipotle peppers and adobo sauce until blended.

3. Grill steaks, covered, over medium heat or broil 3-4 in. from the heat until meat reaches desired doneness (for medium-rare, a thermometer should read 135°; medium, 140°; medium-well, 145°), 5-7 minutes on each side. Serve with chipotle butter.

1 steak with about 1 Tbsp. butter: 860 cal., 66g fat (29g sat. fat), 232mg chol., 1221mg sod., 2g carb. (1g sugars, 1g fiber), 61g pro.

FAST BAKED FISH

We always have a good supply of fresh fish, so I make this dish often. It's moist, tender and flavorful.

—Judie Anglen, Riverton, WY

- -

Takes: 25 min. • **Makes:** 4 servings

1¼ lbs. fish fillets
1 tsp. seasoned salt
Pepper to taste
Paprika, optional
3 Tbsp. butter, melted

1. Preheat oven to 400°. Place fish in a greased 11x7-in. baking dish. Sprinkle with seasoned salt, pepper and, if desired, paprika. Drizzle with melted butter.

2. Cover and bake until fish just begins to flake easily with a fork, 15-20 minutes.

1 serving: 270 cal., 17g fat (7g sat. fat), 110mg chol., 540mg sod., 0 carb. (0 sugars, 0 fiber), 28g pro

FAST BAKED FISH

PEPPER JACK MEAT LOAF

This is a quick way to put a zesty twist on a traditional main dish. The meat loaf is stuffed with pepper jack cheese and has even more melted on top.

—Debra Hartze, Zeeland, ND

- -

Prep: 20 min.
Bake: 55 min. + standing
Makes: 6 servings

1 large egg, lightly beaten
1 cup seasoned bread crumbs
¼ cup chopped onion
½ to 1 tsp. salt
½ tsp. pepper
1½ lbs. lean ground beef (90% lean)
1 cup pepper jack cheese, divided
1 cup salsa, optional

1. In a large bowl, combine the egg, bread crumbs, onion, salt and pepper. Crumble beef over mixture and mix well. Press half of the beef mixture onto the bottom and halfway up the sides of a greased 8x4-in. loaf pan. Sprinkle ¾ cup cheese over meat to within ½ in. of sides. Pat remaining beef mixture over cheese.

2. Bake, uncovered, at 350° for 50-55 minutes or until meat is no longer pink and a thermometer reads 160°. Sprinkle with remaining cheese. Bake 5 minutes longer or until cheese is melted. Let stand for 10 minutes before slicing. Serve with salsa if desired.

1 serving: 331 cal., 16g fat (7g sat. fat), 111mg chol., 681mg sod., 15g carb. (1g sugars, 1g fiber), 30g pro.

PORK CHOPS WITH APPLES & STUFFING

The heartwarming taste of cinnamon and apples is the perfect accompaniment to tender pork chops. This dish is always a winner with my family. Because it calls for only four ingredients, it's a main course I can serve with little preparation.
—Joan Hamilton, Worcester, MA

Prep: 15 min. • **Bake:** 45 min.
Makes: 6 servings

- 6 boneless pork loin chops (6 oz. each)
- 1 Tbsp. canola oil
- 1 pkg. (6 oz.) crushed stuffing mix
- 1 can (21 oz.) apple pie filling with cinnamon
  Minced fresh parsley, optional

1. In a large skillet, brown the pork chops in oil over medium-high heat. Meanwhile, prepare stuffing mix according to package directions. Spread pie filling into a greased 13x9-in. baking dish. Place the pork chops on top; spoon prepared stuffing over chops.

2. Cover and bake at 350° for 35 minutes. Uncover; bake until a thermometer reads 145°, about 10 minutes longer. If desired, sprinkle with parsley.

1 serving: 527 cal., 21g fat (9g sat. fat), 102mg chol., 550mg sod., 48g carb. (15g sugars, 3g fiber), 36g pro.

PORK CHOPS WITH APPLES & STUFFING

SAUCY BAKED
CHICKEN

SAUCY BAKED CHICKEN

This irresistible chicken gets its wonderful flavor from baking in a bubbling mixture of honey and soy sauce. It's always a hit.
—Caroline Champoux,
Londonderry, NH

- -

Prep: 25 min. • **Bake:** 30 min.
Makes: 6 servings

- 6 **boneless skinless chicken breast halves (6 oz. each)**
- 1 **cup honey**
- ½ **cup reduced-sodium soy sauce**
- 2 **Tbsp. olive oil**
- 2 **Tbsp. ketchup**
- 1 **garlic clove, minced**
- ¼ **tsp. salt**
- ⅛ **tsp. pepper**

1. Preheat oven to 375°. Place chicken in a greased 13x9-in. baking dish. In a small bowl, mix the remaining ingredients; pour over chicken.

2. Bake, uncovered, 30-35 minutes or until thermometer inserted in chicken reads 165°, basting occasionally. Remove chicken from dish and keep warm.

3. Transfer sauce to a small saucepan. Bring to a boil; cook and stir 12-15 minutes or until sauce is reduced to 1¼ cups.

Freeze option: Cover and freeze cooled chicken and sauce in freezer containers. To use, partially thaw in refrigerator overnight. Reheat in a foil-lined 13x9-in. baking dish in a preheated 325° oven until heated through, covering if necessary to prevent excess browning.

1 chicken breast half with about 3 Tbsp. sauce: 412 cal., 8g fat (2g sat. fat), 94mg chol., 1013mg sod., 49g carb. (47g sugars, 0 fiber), 36g pro.

**ARTICHOKE CHICKEN
PESTO PIZZA**

ARTICHOKE CHICKEN PESTO PIZZA

Make pizza night an upscale affair with this fun twist on the traditional pie. A prebaked crust and prepared pesto keep things quick and easy.

—Trisha Kruse, Eagle, ID

- -

Takes: 15 min. • **Makes:** 8 servings

- 1   prebaked 12-in. pizza crust
- ½   cup prepared pesto
- 2   cups cubed cooked chicken breast
- 2   jars (6½ oz. each) marinated artichoke hearts, drained
- 2   cups shredded part-skim mozzarella cheese
    Optional: Grated Parmesan cheese and minced fresh basil

Preheat oven to 425°. Place crust on an ungreased 12-in. pizza pan. Spread with pesto. Arrange chicken and artichokes over top; sprinkle with cheese. Bake until golden brown, 10-12 minutes. If desired, top with Parmesan cheese and minced fresh basil.

1 piece: 381 cal., 20g fat (6g sat. fat), 45mg chol., 880mg sod., 28g carb. (2g sugars, 4g fiber), 23g pro.

★ ★ ★ ★ ★ **READER REVIEW**

"Fantastic. So easy to put together and yummy. I always have the ingredients ready. I buy ready-made pesto from our market's salad bar."

—FERRYAL, TASTEOFHOME.COM

EASY SLOW-COOKED SWISS STEAK

EASY SLOW-COOKED SWISS STEAK

Let your slow cooker simmer up this fuss-free and flavorful Swiss steak. It's perfect for busy days. The longer it cooks, the better it tastes!

—Sarah Burks, Wathena, KS

- -

Prep: 10 min. • **Cook:** 6 hours
Makes: 2 servings

- 1   Tbsp. all-purpose flour
- ¼   tsp. salt
- ⅛   tsp. pepper
- ¾   lb. beef top round steak
- ½   medium onion, cut into ¼-in. slices
- ⅓   cup chopped celery
- 1   can (8 oz.) tomato sauce

1. In a large shallow dish, combine the flour, salt and pepper. Cut beef into 2 portions; add to dish and turn to coat.

2. Place onion in a 3-qt. slow cooker coated with cooking spray. Layer with the beef, celery and tomato sauce. Cover; cook on low 6-8 hours or until meat is tender.

1 serving: 272 cal., 5g fat (2g sat. fat), 96mg chol., 882mg sod., 13g carb. (4g sugars, 2g fiber), 41g pro.

RASPBERRY CHICKEN

Basic skillet-cooked chicken gets a slightly sweet kick with this fresh, fun raspberry sauce, and it's scrumptious over rice, too.

—Anita Hennesy, Hagerstown, MD

- -

Takes: 30 min. • **Makes:** 4 servings

  4 boneless skinless chicken breast halves (5 oz. each)
  ¼ tsp. salt
  ¼ tsp. pepper
  ½ cup seedless raspberry jam
  2 Tbsp. balsamic vinegar
  1 Tbsp. reduced-sodium soy sauce
  ⅛ tsp. crushed red pepper flakes

1. Sprinkle chicken with salt and pepper. In a large skillet coated with cooking spray, cook chicken over medium heat for 5-7 minutes on each side or until a thermometer reads 165°.

2. Meanwhile, in a small saucepan, combine the remaining ingredients. Bring to a boil; cook until liquid is reduced to ½ cup. Serve sauce with chicken.

1 serving: 260 cal., 3g fat (1g sat. fat), 78mg chol., 369mg sod., 28g carb. (25g sugars, 0 fiber), 29g pro.
Diabetic exchanges: 4 lean meat, 1½ starch.

WEEKNIGHT RAVIOLI LASAGNA

My husband and I love lasagna, but it's time-consuming to build and we always end up with too much. Using frozen ravioli solves everything.

—Pamela Nicholson, Festus, MO

- -

Prep: 15 min. • **Bake:** 45 min.
Makes: 6 servings

  1 jar (24 oz.) pasta sauce
  1 pkg. (25 oz.) frozen meat or cheese ravioli
  1½ cups shredded part-skim mozzarella cheese
  3 cups fresh baby spinach

1. Preheat oven to 350°. In a small saucepan, heat sauce 5-7 minutes over medium heat or just until simmering, stirring occasionally.

2. Spread ½ cup sauce into a greased 11x7-in. baking dish. Layer with half the ravioli, 1½ cups spinach, ½ cup cheese and half of the remaining sauce; repeat layers. Sprinkle with remaining cheese.

3. Bake, uncovered, 45-50 minutes or until edges are bubbly and cheese is melted. Let stand for 5 minutes before serving.

1 cup: 344 cal., 10g fat (5g sat. fat), 26mg chol., 850mg sod., 45g carb. (10g sugars, 5g fiber), 17g pro.
Diabetic exchanges: 3 starch, 2 medium-fat meat.

WEEKNIGHT RAVIOLI LASAGNA

**GINGER-GLAZED
GRILLED SALMON**

GINGER-GLAZED GRILLED SALMON

Our family loves to have salmon prepared this way, and it's a real treat to make on a warm summer evening. These fillets also may be baked in the oven at 450° for 18 minutes, basting occasionally.
—Wanda Toews, Cromer, MB

- -

Takes: 15 min. • **Makes:** 4 servings

2 Tbsp. reduced-sodium
  soy sauce
2 Tbsp. maple syrup
2 tsp. minced fresh gingerroot
2 garlic cloves, minced
4 salmon fillets (6 oz. each)

1. For glaze, mix first 4 ingredients.
2. Place salmon on an oiled grill rack over medium heat, skin side up. Grill, covered, until fish just begins to flake easily with a fork, 4-5 minutes per side; brush top with half of the glaze after turning. Brush with remaining glaze before serving.

1 fillet: 299 cal., 16g fat (3g sat. fat), 85mg chol., 374mg sod., 8g carb. (6g sugars, 0 fiber), 29g pro.
Diabetic exchanges: 4 lean meat, ½ starch.

BUTTERY PARMESAN CHICKEN

BUTTERY PARMESAN CHICKEN

A rich, cheesy breading locks in chicken's natural juices, making this dish moist and tempting every time. Because it can be made in advance, I often rely on it during the week and also when I'm entertaining.

—Kathie Landmann, Lexington Park, MD

- -

Takes: 30 min. • **Makes:** 6 servings

1 cup grated Parmesan cheese
2 cups soft bread crumbs
½ cup butter, melted
6 boneless skinless chicken breast halves (6 oz. each)
½ cup Dijon, yellow or country-style mustard

Combine Parmesan cheese, bread crumbs and butter. Coat chicken with mustard, then dip into crumb mixture. Place chicken in a 13x9-in. baking pan. Bake at 425° until a thermometer inserted in chicken reads 165°, about 15 minutes.

Note: To make soft bread crumbs, tear bread into pieces and place in a food processor or blender. Cover and pulse until crumbs form. One slice of bread yields ½-¾ cup crumbs.

1 chicken breast half: 391 cal., 24g fat (13g sat. fat), 119mg chol., 1047mg sod., 10g carb. (1g sugars, 1g fiber), 33g pro.

BEAN BURRITOS

I always have the ingredients for this cheesy bean burrito recipe on hand. Cooking the rice and shredding the cheese the night before save precious minutes at dinnertime.

—Beth Osborne Skinner, Bristol, TN

- -

Takes: 30 min. • **Makes:** 6 servings

1 **can (16 oz.) refried beans**
1 **cup salsa**
1 **cup cooked long grain rice**
2 **cups shredded cheddar cheese, divided**
12 **flour tortillas (6 in.)**
   Shredded lettuce, optional

1. Preheat oven to 375°. In a large bowl, combine beans, salsa, rice and 1 cup cheese. Spoon about ⅓ cup off-center on each tortilla. Fold the sides and ends over filling and roll up.
2. Arrange burritos in a greased 13x9-in. baking dish. Sprinkle with remaining 1 cup cheese. Cover and bake until heated through, 20-25 minutes. If desired, top with lettuce.

2 burritos: 216 cal., 9g fat (4g sat. fat), 23mg chol., 544mg sod., 24g carb. (1g sugars, 3g fiber), 9g pro.

BEAN BURRITOS

GRILLED RIBEYES WITH BROWNED GARLIC BUTTER

GRILLED RIBEYES WITH BROWNED GARLIC BUTTER

Use the grill's smoke to flavor the ribeyes, then slather them with garlicky butter for a standout entree your friends and family will always remember.

—Arge Salvatori, Waldwick, NJ

Takes: 25 min. • **Makes:** 8 servings

- 6 Tbsp. unsalted butter, cubed
- 2 garlic cloves, minced
- 4 beef ribeye steaks (about 1 in. thick and 12 oz. each)
- 1½ tsp. salt
- 1½ tsp. pepper

1. In a small heavy saucepan, melt butter with garlic over medium heat. Heat 4-6 minutes or until butter is golden brown, stirring constantly. Remove from heat.

2. Season the steaks with salt and pepper. Grill, covered, over medium heat or broil 4 in. from heat for 5-7 minutes on each side or until meat reaches desired doneness (for medium-rare, a thermometer should read 135°; medium, 140°; medium-well, 145°).

3. Gently warm garlic butter over low heat. Serve with steaks.

4 oz. cooked beef with 2 tsp. garlic butter: 449 cal., 36g fat (16g sat. fat), 123mg chol., 521mg sod., 1g carb. (0 sugars, 0 fiber), 30g pro.

ROSEMARY LIME CHICKEN

I experimented quite a bit before creating the tasty final version of this entree.

—Nicole Harris, Mount Union, PA

Takes: 20 min. • **Makes:** 4 servings

- 4 boneless skinless chicken breast halves (5 oz. each)
- 2 Tbsp. canola oil
- ½ cup white wine or chicken broth
- ¼ cup lime juice
- 2 Tbsp. minced fresh rosemary or 2 tsp. dried rosemary, crushed
- ½ tsp. salt
- ¼ tsp. pepper

Flatten chicken to ½-in. thickness. In a large skillet, brown chicken in oil over medium-high heat. Add the remaining ingredients. Cook, uncovered, until chicken is no longer pink, 5-7 minutes.

1 serving: 244 cal., 9g fat (1g sat. fat), 82mg chol., 389mg sod., 2g carb. (0 sugars, 1g fiber), 33g pro. **Diabetic exchanges:** 4 lean meat, ½ fat.

★ ★ ★ ★ ★ **READER REVIEW**

"Lime and rosemary are great together. My husband especially liked it! I recommend a mild side dish to balance the chicken."

—TAMMYCOOKBLOGSBOOKS, TASTEOFHOME.COM

ROSEMARY LIME
CHICKEN

CAPRESE
CHICKEN WITH
BACON

CAPRESE CHICKEN WITH BACON

Smoky bacon, fresh basil, ripe tomatoes and gooey mozzarella top these appealing chicken breasts. The aroma as the chicken bakes is irresistible!
—Tammy Hayden, Quincy, MI

Prep: 20 min. • **Bake:** 15 min.
Makes: 4 servings

- 8 **bacon strips**
- 4 **boneless skinless chicken breast halves (6 oz. each)**
- 1 **Tbsp. olive oil**
- ½ **tsp. salt**
- ¼ **tsp. pepper**
- 2 **plum tomatoes, sliced**
- 6 **fresh basil leaves, thinly sliced**
- 4 **slices part-skim mozzarella cheese**

1. Preheat oven to 400°. Place bacon in an ungreased 15x10x1-in. baking pan. Bake until partially cooked but not crisp, 8-10 minutes. Remove to paper towels to drain.

2. Place chicken in an ungreased 13x9-in. baking pan; brush with oil and sprinkle with salt and pepper. Top with tomatoes and basil. Wrap each in 2 bacon strips, arranging bacon in a crisscross.

3. Bake chicken, uncovered, until a thermometer reads 165°, 15-20 minutes. Top with cheese; bake until melted, 1 minute longer.

1 chicken breast half: 373 cal., 18g fat (7g sat. fat), 123mg chol., 821mg sod., 3g carb. (1g sugars, 0 fiber), 47g pro.

SLOW-COOKER KALUA PORK & CABBAGE

My slow-cooker pork has four ingredients and takes less than 10 minutes to prep. The result tastes exactly like the Kalua pork made in Hawaii that's slow-roasted all day in an underground oven.

—Rholinelle DeTorres, San Jose, CA

Prep: 10 min. • **Cook:** 9 hours
Makes: 12 servings

- 7 bacon strips, divided
- 1 boneless pork shoulder butt roast (3 to 4 lbs.), well trimmed
- 1 Tbsp. coarse sea salt
- 1 medium head cabbage (about 2 lbs.), coarsely chopped

1. Line bottom of a 6-qt. slow cooker with 4 bacon strips. Sprinkle all sides of roast with salt; place in slow cooker. Arrange remaining bacon over top of roast.

2. Cook, covered, on low 8-10 hours or until pork is tender. Add cabbage, spreading cabbage around roast. Cook, covered, 1-1¼ hours longer or until cabbage is tender.

3. Remove pork to a serving bowl; shred pork with 2 forks. Using a slotted spoon, add cabbage to pork and toss to combine. If desired, skim fat from some of the cooking juices; stir juices into pork mixture or serve on the side.

1 cup: 227 cal., 13g fat (5g sat. fat), 72mg chol., 622mg sod., 4g carb. (2g sugars, 2g fiber), 22g pro.

SPICY CHICKEN NUGGETS

We devour these golden brown chicken nuggets at least once a week. If you want to tone down the heat a bit, just skip the chipotle pepper.

—Cheryl Cook, Palmyra, VA

Takes: 30 min. • **Makes:** 6 servings

- 1½ cups panko bread crumbs
- 1½ cups grated Parmesan cheese
- ½ tsp. ground chipotle pepper, optional
- ¼ cup butter, melted
- 1½ lbs. boneless skinless chicken thighs, cut into 1½-in. pieces

1. Preheat oven to 400°. In a shallow bowl, mix bread crumbs, cheese and, if desired, chipotle pepper. Place butter in a separate shallow bowl. Dip chicken pieces in butter, then in crumb mixture, patting to help coating adhere.

2. Place chicken on a greased 15x10x1-in. baking pan; sprinkle with remaining crumb mixture. Bake 20-25 minutes or until no longer pink.

1 serving: 371 cal., 22g fat (10g sat. fat), 113mg chol., 527mg sod., 13g carb. (1g sugars, 1g fiber), 29g pro.

SLOW-COOKER KALUA
PORK & CABBAGE

SUPER EASY COUNTRY-STYLE RIBS

I'm a die-hard ribs fan. When we were growing up, our mom made these for us all the time, and we still can't get enough of them.

—Stephanie Loaiza, Layton, UT

- -

Prep: 10 min. • **Cook:** 5 hours
Makes: 4 servings

- 1½ cups ketchup
- ½ cup packed brown sugar
- ½ cup white vinegar
- 2 tsp. seasoned salt
- ½ tsp. liquid smoke, optional
- 2 lbs. boneless country-style pork ribs

1. In a 3-qt. slow cooker, mix ketchup, brown sugar, vinegar, seasoned salt and, if desired, liquid smoke. Add ribs; turn to coat. Cook, covered, on low 5-6 hours or until meat is tender.

2. Remove pork to a serving plate. Skim fat from cooking liquid. If desired, transfer to a small saucepan to thicken; bring to a boil and cook 12-15 minutes or until sauce is reduced to 1½ cups. Serve with ribs.

To make ahead: In a large airtight container, combine ketchup, brown sugar, vinegar, seasoned salt and, if desired, liquid smoke. Add pork; cover and freeze. To use, place container in refrigerator 48 hours or until ribs are completely thawed. Cook as directed.

6 oz. cooked pork with about ⅓ cup sauce: 550 cal., 21g fat (8g sat. fat), 131mg chol., 2003mg sod., 51g carb. (51g sugars, 0 fiber), 40g pro.

**SUPER EASY
COUNTRY-STYLE RIBS**

CRANBERRY MAPLE
CHICKEN

CRANBERRY MAPLE CHICKEN

Cranberries and a hint of maple syrup make a sweet sauce for these easy chicken breast halves. They're a quick but lovely main course for weeknights and other occasions.

—Kim Pettipas, Oromocto, NB

- -

Takes: 30 min. • **Makes:** 6 servings

- 2 **cups fresh or frozen cranberries**
- ¾ **cup water**
- ⅓ **cup sugar**
- 6 **boneless skinless chicken breast halves (4 oz. each)**
- ½ **tsp. salt**
- ¼ **tsp. pepper**
- 1 **Tbsp. canola oil**
- ¼ **cup maple syrup**

1. In a small saucepan, combine the cranberries, water and sugar. Cook over medium heat until berries pop, about 15 minutes.

2. Meanwhile, sprinkle chicken with salt and pepper. In a large nonstick skillet, cook chicken in oil over medium heat until juices run clear, 4-5 minutes on each side. Stir syrup into the cranberry mixture; serve with chicken.

1 chicken breast half with 3 Tbsp. sauce: 236 cal., 5g fat (1g sat. fat), 63mg chol., 253mg sod., 24g carb. (22g sugars, 1g fiber), 23g pro.

SPECIAL PORK
CHOPS

SPECIAL PORK CHOPS

I work nine hours a day, so I need delicious and simple recipes like this one. My husband thinks I work hard fixing meals, but these chops are good and easy. In summer, I can my own salsa and use some to top these chops.
—LaDane Wilson, Alexander City, AL

- -

Takes: 30 min. • **Makes:** 6 servings

- 6 **boneless pork chops (6 oz. each)**
- 1 **Tbsp. canola oil**
- 1 **jar (16 oz.) salsa**

In a large cast-iron or other ovenproof skillet, brown the pork chops in oil; drain any fat. Pour salsa over chops. Bake, uncovered, at 350° until a thermometer reads 145°, 20-25 minutes. Let stand for 5 minutes.

1 pork chop: 273 cal., 12g fat (4g sat. fat), 82mg chol., 350mg sod., 5g carb. (3g sugars, 0 fiber), 33g pro. **Diabetic exchanges:** 5 lean meat, ½ fat.

LEMON CHICKEN BAKE

LEMON CHICKEN BAKE

This lovely chicken is as good cold as it is right out of the oven. It's moist, tender and lemony with a nice crunch. It's a delicious picnic entree as well as a wonderful meal with scalloped or baked potatoes and a fresh green salad on the side.
—Marion Lowery, Medford, OR

- -

Prep: 10 min. • **Bake:** 25 min.
Makes: 4 servings

- 3 **Tbsp. butter, melted**
- 2 **Tbsp. lemon juice**
- 1 **garlic clove, minced**
- ½ **tsp. salt**
- ¼ **tsp. pepper**
- ½ **cup seasoned bread crumbs**
- 4 **boneless skinless chicken breast halves (6 oz. each)**

1. Preheat oven to 350°. In a shallow dish, combine butter, lemon juice, garlic, salt and pepper. Place bread crumbs in another dish. Dip chicken in butter mixture, then coat with bread crumbs.

2. Place in a greased 13x9-in. baking dish. Drizzle with remaining butter mixture. Bake, uncovered, until a thermometer inserted in chicken reads 165°, 25-30 minutes.

1 serving: 255 cal., 12g fat (6g sat. fat), 86mg chol., 652mg sod., 11g carb. (1g sugars, 1g fiber), 25g pro.

SUPER SPAGHETTI SAUCE

At my house, we never know how many we'll have for dinner. That's why this spaghetti sauce is one of my favorites—it's flavorful, filling and fast. Smoked kielbasa gives it depth, and salsa adds the kick.

—Bella Anderson, Chester, SC

- - - - - - - - - - - - - - - - - - - -

Takes: 30 min. • **Makes:** 2½ qt.

- 1 **lb. ground beef**
- 1 **lb. smoked kielbasa, cut into ¼-in. slices**
- 2 **jars (24 oz. each) spaghetti sauce with mushrooms**
- 1 **jar (16 oz.) chunky salsa**
  Hot cooked pasta

1. In a Dutch oven, cook beef over medium heat until no longer pink; drain and set aside. In the same pan, cook sausage over medium heat for 5-6 minutes or until browned.

2. Stir in the spaghetti sauce, salsa and reserved beef; heat through. Serve with pasta.

1 cup: 325 cal., 21g fat (7g sat. fat), 60mg chol., 1378mg sod., 18g carb. (11g sugars, 2g fiber), 17g pro.

GRILLED PINEAPPLE CHICKEN

A trip to Hawaii is easy with this juicy grilled pineapple chicken. Simply give it a quick marinade, fire up the grill and let it sizzle. We love this low-carb recipe!

—Charlotte Rogers, Va Beach, VA

- - - - - - - - - - - - - - - - - - - -

Prep: 10 min. + marinating
Grill: 10 min. • **Makes:** 4 servings

- ¼ **cup unsweetened pineapple juice**
- 2 **Tbsp. sherry**
- 2 **Tbsp. soy sauce**
- ¼ **tsp. ground ginger**
  Dash salt
  Dash pepper
- 4 **boneless skinless chicken breast halves (6 oz. each)**
  Optional: Grilled pineapple and sliced green onions

1. In a large bowl, combine the first 6 ingredients; add chicken and turn to coat. Cover and refrigerate for 1-2 hours.

2. Drain and discard marinade. Grill chicken, covered, over medium heat or broil 4 in. from the heat for 5-7 minutes on each side or until a meat thermometer reads 165°. If desired, serve with grilled pineapple and sliced green onions.

1 serving: 187 cal., 4g fat (1g sat. fat), 94mg chol., 209mg sod., 1g carb. (0 sugars, 0 fiber), 35g pro. **Diabetic exchanges:** 5 lean meat.

GRILLED PINEAPPLE CHICKEN

MERLOT FILET MIGNON

Although this filet is made simply, you can feel confident serving it to guests. The rich sauce adds a touch of elegance. To round out the meal, just add a salad and dinner rolls.

—Jauneen Hosking, Waterford, WI

Takes: 20 min. • **Makes:** 2 servings

- 2 **beef tenderloin steaks (8 oz. each)**
- 3 **Tbsp. butter, divided**
- 1 **Tbsp. olive oil**
- 1 **cup merlot**
- 2 **Tbsp. heavy whipping cream**
- ⅛ **tsp. salt**

1. In a small skillet, cook steaks in 1 Tbsp. butter and the olive oil over medium heat until meat reaches desired doneness (for medium-rare, a thermometer should read 135°; medium, 140°; medium-well, 145°), 4-6 minutes on each side. Remove and keep warm.

2. In the same skillet, add wine, stirring to loosen browned bits from pan. Bring to a boil; cook until liquid is reduced to ¼ cup. Add the cream, salt and remaining butter; bring to a boil. Cook and stir until sauce is slightly thickened and butter is melted, 1-2 minutes. Serve sauce with steaks.

1 steak with 2 Tbsp. sauce: 690 cal., 43g fat (20g sat. fat), 165mg chol., 279mg sod., 4g carb. (1g sugars, 0 fiber), 49g pro.

SLAMMIN' LAMB

SLAMMIN' LAMB

This meat is easy, flavorful and best when marinated overnight. You can even mix it up and freeze it until you want to throw it in the crock! Make sure you have lots of pita bread on hand to soak up the juices.

—Ruth Hartunian-Alumbaugh, Willimantic, CT

Prep: 20 min. + marinating
Cook: 4 hours • **Makes:** 6 servings

- 2   **small garlic bulbs**
- ¾   **cup plus 2 Tbsp. minced fresh mint, divided**
- ½   **cup balsamic vinegar**
- ¼   **cup olive oil**
- 2   **lbs. boneless lamb, cut into 1-in. cubes**
     Hot cooked rice or pita bread, optional

1. Remove papery outer skin from garlic bulbs; cut off tops of bulbs, exposing individual cloves. Peel and halve cloves. In a large dish, combine garlic, ¾ cup mint, vinegar and olive oil. Add lamb; turn to coat. Cover and refrigerate up to 24 hours.

2. Transfer lamb and marinade to a 3-qt. slow cooker. Cook, covered, on low 4-5 hours or until meat is tender. Sprinkle with remaining mint; if desired, serve with hot cooked rice or pita bread.

1 serving: 323 cal., 17g fat (4g sat. fat), 98mg chol., 102mg sod., 10g carb. (6g sugars, 1g fiber), 31g pro.

RAVIOLI CASSEROLE

The whole family will love this yummy dish that tastes like lasagna without all the fuss. Timesaving ingredients like prepared spaghetti sauce and frozen ravioli make it a cinch to make. Children can help you assemble this one.

—Mary Ann Rothert, Austin, TX

Prep: 10 min. • **Bake:** 30 min.
Makes: 8 servings

- 1 pkg. (20 oz.) refrigerated cheese ravioli
- 3½ cups pasta sauce
- 2 cups small-curd 4% cottage cheese
- 4 cups shredded mozzarella cheese
- ¼ cup grated Parmesan cheese
  Minced fresh parsley, optional

1. Preheat the oven to 350°. Prepare cheese ravioli according to package directions; drain. Spread 1 cup spaghetti sauce in an ungreased 13x9-in. baking dish. Layer with half of the ravioli, 1¼ cups sauce, 1 cup cottage cheese and 2 cups of the mozzarella cheese. Repeat layers. Sprinkle with Parmesan cheese.

2. Bake, uncovered, until bubbly, 30-40 minutes. Let stand 5-10 minutes before serving. If desired, sprinkle with parsley.

1 cup: 518 cal., 25g fat (12g sat. fat), 88mg chol., 1411mg sod., 44g carb. (13g sugars, 5g fiber), 30g pro.

RAVIOLI
CASSEROLE

**SCALLOPS
IN SAGE CREAM**

PARMESAN PORK MEDALLIONS

I was so happy to find this recipe. I have served it countless times for family and friends. It takes very little prep time and adapts easily to serve any number.
—Angela Ciocca, Saltsburg, PA

- -

Takes: 20 min. • **Makes:** 2 servings

½	**lb. pork tenderloin**
2	**Tbsp. seasoned bread crumbs**
1	**Tbsp. grated Parmesan cheese**
¼	**tsp. salt**
	Dash pepper
2	**tsp. canola oil**
¼	**cup sliced onion**
1	**garlic clove, minced**

1. Cut pork into 4 slices; flatten to ¼-in. thickness. In a large shallow dish, combine the bread crumbs, cheese, salt and pepper. Add pork, 1 slice at a time, and turn to coat.
2. In a large skillet over medium heat, cook pork in oil until meat is no longer pink, 2-3 minutes on each side. Remove and keep warm.
3. Add onion to the pan; cook and stir until tender. Add garlic, cook 1 minute longer. Serve with pork.
1 serving: 220 cal., 9g fat (2g sat. fat), 65mg chol., 487mg sod., 8g carb. (1g sugars, 1g fiber), 25g pro.
Diabetic exchanges: 3 lean meat, 1 fat, ½ starch.

SCALLOPS IN SAGE CREAM

I didn't want to hide the ocean freshness of the scallops that I bought on the dock from a local fisherman, so I used some simple ingredients to showcase them.
—Joan Churchill, Dover, NH

- -

Takes: 20 min. • **Makes:** 4 servings

1½	**lbs. sea scallops**
¼	**tsp. salt**
⅛	**tsp. pepper**
3	**Tbsp. olive oil, divided**
½	**cup chopped shallots**
¾	**cup heavy whipping cream**
6	**fresh sage leaves, thinly sliced**
	Hot cooked pasta, optional

1. Sprinkle scallops with salt and pepper. In a large skillet, cook scallops in 2 Tbsp. oil until firm and opaque, 1½-2 minutes on each side. Remove and keep warm.
2. In the same skillet, saute the shallots in remaining oil until tender. Add cream; bring to a boil. Cook and stir for 30 seconds or until slightly thickened.
3. Return scallops to the pan; heat through. Stir in sage. Serve with pasta if desired.
1 serving: 408 cal., 28g fat (12g sat. fat), 117mg chol., 441mg sod., 9g carb. (1g sugars, 0 fiber), 30g pro.

PARMESAN PORK
MEDALLIONS

**CONTEST-WINNING
BARBECUED PORK CHOPS**

CONTEST-WINNING BARBECUED PORK CHOPS

Sherry, honey, barbecue and steak sauces combine to give these chops a beautiful glaze and dressed-up flavor. The sauce works very well on chicken breasts, too.

—LaJuana Kay Holland, Amarillo, TX

Takes: 20 min. • **Makes:** 6 servings

⅓ cup hickory smoke-flavored barbecue sauce
⅓ cup A.1. steak sauce
⅓ cup sherry or unsweetened apple juice
2 Tbsp. honey
6 bone-in pork loin chops (¾ in. thick and 8 oz. each)
¾ tsp. salt
½ tsp. pepper

1. Mix first 4 ingredients; reserve ⅓ cup sauce for serving.

2. Sprinkle pork chops with salt and pepper. Place on an oiled grill rack over medium heat. Grill, covered, until a thermometer reads 145°, 4-6 minutes per side, brushing frequently with remaining sauce after turning. Let stand 5 minutes before serving. Serve with the reserved sauce.

1 pork chop with 2 tsp. sauce: 299 cal., 10g fat (4g sat. fat), 98mg chol., 771mg sod., 16g carb. (14g sugars, 0 fiber), 35g pro.

ALOHA PIZZA

This pizza came together on the fly. I had to take something to a gathering, but had no time to shop. I raided the fridge for inspiration and discovered this happy combo.

—Wendy Huffman, Bloomington, IL

- -

Takes: 30 min. • **Makes:** 6 pieces

- 1 **tube (8 oz.) refrigerated crescent rolls**
- ½ **cup honey barbecue sauce**
- 1 **pkg. (6 oz.) ready-to-use grilled chicken breast strips**
- 1 **cup pineapple tidbits**
- 1½ **cups shredded Mexican cheese blend**

1. Unroll crescent dough into a greased 13x9-in. baking pan; seal seams and perforations. Bake at 375° until crust is golden brown, 6-8 minutes.

2. Spread sauce over crust. Top with chicken, pineapple and cheese. Bake pizza until cheese is melted, 12-15 minutes longer.

1 piece: 351 cal., 18g fat (8g sat. fat), 44mg chol., 985mg sod., 29g carb. (14g sugars, 0 fiber), 15g pro.

TEST KITCHEN TIP
If you have leftover chicken on hand, use 1½-2 cups cubed or shredded meat instead of the grilled strips. Shredded Monterey Jack or mozzarella cheese would taste great on this pizza.

PEPPERED PORTOBELLO PENNE

Hearty mushrooms and a kickin' hot cheese sauce take this simple pasta toss from drab to fab! My family loves the fact that it tastes like a restaurant dish but is made at home.

—Veronica Callaghan, Glastonbury, CT

- -

Takes: 30 min. • **Makes:** 4 servings

- 2 **cups uncooked penne pasta**
- 4 **large portobello mushrooms, stems removed, halved and thinly sliced**
- 2 **Tbsp. olive oil**
- ½ **cup heavy whipping cream**
- ¾ **tsp. salt**
- ¼ **tsp. pepper**
- 1 **cup shredded pepper jack cheese**

1. Cook pasta according to the package directions.

2. Meanwhile, in a large skillet, saute mushrooms in oil until tender. Stir in the cream, salt and pepper; heat through. Stir in pepper jack cheese until melted. Drain pasta. Add to skillet and toss to coat.

1 cup: 503 cal., 28g fat (13g sat. fat), 71mg chol., 632mg sod., 48g carb. (3g sugars, 3g fiber), 17g pro.

ALOHA PIZZA

TORTELLINI WITH SAUSAGE & MASCARPONE

TORTELLINI WITH SAUSAGE & MASCARPONE

When I crave Italian comfort food on a busy night and don't have a lot of time to cook, this dish is fast and yummy. You can have it on the table in less time than a takeout order.

—Gerry Vance, Millbrae, CA

- -

Takes: 20 min. • **Makes:** 6 servings

- 1   pkg. (20 oz.) refrigerated cheese tortellini
- 8   oz. bulk Italian sausage
- 1   jar (24 oz.) pasta sauce with mushrooms
- ½   cup shredded Parmesan cheese
- 1   carton (8 oz.) mascarpone cheese
    Crushed red pepper flakes, optional

1. Prepare tortellini according to package directions. Meanwhile, in a large cast-iron or other heavy skillet, cook sausage over medium heat until no longer pink, 6-8 minutes, breaking into crumbles; drain. Stir in pasta sauce; heat through.

2. Drain tortellini, reserving 1 cup cooking water. Add tortellini to sauce with enough reserved cooking water to reach desired consistency; toss to coat. Stir in Parmesan cheese; dollop with mascarpone cheese. If desired, sprinkle with red pepper flakes.

1 cup: 637 cal., 37g fat (17g sat. fat), 113mg chol., 1040mg sod., 57g carb. (11g sugars, 4g fiber), 24g pro.

BLACK BEAN
& BEEF TOSTADAS

*You only need a handful of
ingredients to make one of our
family's favorites. It's also easy
to double for company!*

—Susan Brown, Kansas City, KS

- -

Takes: 30 min. • **Makes:** 4 servings

½ **lb. lean ground beef
(90% lean)**
1 **can (10 oz.) diced tomatoes
and green chiles, undrained**

1 **can (15 oz.) black beans,
rinsed and drained**
1 **can (16 oz.) refried beans,
warmed**
8 **tostada shells
Optional toppings: Shredded
reduced-fat Mexican cheese
blend, shredded lettuce, salsa
and sour cream**

1. In a large skillet, cook and crumble
beef over medium-high heat until no
longer pink, 4-6 minutes. Stir in
tomatoes; bring to a boil. Reduce
heat; simmer, uncovered, until liquid
is almost evaporated, 6-8 minutes.
Stir in black beans; heat through.
2. To serve, spread refried beans
over tostada shells. Top with beef
mixture; add toppings as desired.
2 tostadas: 392 cal., 14g fat (4g sat.
fat), 35mg chol., 1011mg sod., 46g
carb. (2g sugars, 10g fiber), 23g pro.

BEST-EVER LAMB CHOPS

BEST-EVER LAMB CHOPS

My mom just loved a good lamb chop, and this easy recipe was her favorite way to have them. I've also grilled these chops with great results.

—Kim Mundy, Visalia, CA

- -

Prep: 10 min. + chilling
Broil: 10 min. • **Makes:** 4 servings

- 1 tsp. each dried basil, marjoram and thyme
- ½ tsp. salt
- 8 lamb loin chops (3 oz. each)
  Mint jelly, optional

1. Combine herbs and salt; rub over lamb chops. Cover and refrigerate for 1 hour.
2. Broil 4-6 in. from heat until chops reach desired doneness, 5-8 minutes on each side (for medium-rare, a thermometer should read 135°; medium, 140°; medium-well, 145°). Serve with mint jelly if desired.

2 lamb chops: 157 cal., 7g fat (2g sat. fat), 68mg chol., 355mg sod., 0 carb. (0 sugars, 0 fiber), 22g pro. **Diabetic exchanges:** 3 lean meat.

Honey-Glazed Lamb Chops: Omit herbs, salt and step 1. In a saucepan over medium-low heat, combine ⅓ cup each honey and prepared mustard and ⅛ tsp. each onion salt and pepper. Cook until the honey is melted, 2-3 minutes. Brush sauce over both sides of lamb. Broil as directed.

SLOW-COOKED ENCHILADA CASSEROLE

SLOW-COOKED ENCHILADA CASSEROLE

Tortilla chips and a simple side salad turn this casserole into a fun and festive meal with very little effort.

—Denise Waller, Omaha, NE

- -

Prep: 20 min. • **Cook:** 6 hours
Makes: 6 servings

- 1 lb. ground beef
- 2 cans (10 oz. each) enchilada sauce
- 1 can (10¾ oz.) condensed cream of onion soup, undiluted
- ¼ tsp. salt
- 1 pkg. (8½ oz.) flour tortillas, torn
- 3 cups shredded cheddar cheese

1. In a skillet, cook beef over medium heat until no longer pink; drain. Stir in enchilada sauce, soup and salt.
2. In a 3-qt. slow cooker, layer a third of the beef mixture, tortillas and cheese. Repeat the layers twice. Cover and cook on low 6-8 hours or until heated through.

1 serving: 568 cal., 35g fat (16g sat. fat), 105mg chol., 1610mg sod., 30g carb. (4g sugars, 3g fiber), 31g pro.

MOIST TURKEY BREAST

My family always requests this turkey at gatherings. The Italian dressing adds zip that you don't find in other recipes. If you'd like, you can make a flavorful gravy from the pan drippings.
—Cindy Carlson, Ingleside, TX

- -

Prep: 10 min.
Bake: 2 hours + standing
Makes: 14 servings

1	bone-in turkey breast (about 7 lbs.)
1	tsp. garlic powder
½	tsp. onion powder
½	tsp. salt
¼	tsp. pepper
1½	cups Italian dressing

1. Place turkey breast in a greased 13x9-in. baking dish. Combine the seasonings; sprinkle over turkey. Pour dressing over the top.
2. Cover turkey and bake at 325° until a thermometer reads 170°, 2-2½ hours, basting occasionally with pan drippings. Let stand for 10 minutes before slicing.

6 oz. cooked turkey: 406 cal., 22g fat (5g sat. fat), 122mg chol., 621mg sod., 2g carb. (1g sugars, 0 fiber), 47g pro.

Roasted Turkey: Combine 1¾ tsp. garlic powder, ¾ tsp. each onion powder and salt, and ½ tsp. pepper; sprinkle over a 12- to 14-lb. turkey. Place in a roasting pan; top with 2½ cups Italian dressing. Cover; bake at 325° until a thermometer inserted in thigh reads 180°, 3-3½ hours, basting occasionally with the pan drippings. Let stand 20 minutes before carving.

KALUA PORK

Planning a luau-themed party? Then this is the perfect main dish for your get-together. It will feed a crowd, it's easy to prepare, and everyone loves it. Cleanup is a breeze, too! A Hawaiian friend shared this recipe with me while I was stationed in Pearl Harbor several years ago.
—Becky Friedman, Hammond, LA

- -

Prep: 10 min. • **Cook:** 8 hours
Makes: 18 servings

1	boneless pork shoulder roast (5 to 6 lbs.)
1	Tbsp. liquid smoke
4	tsp. sea salt (preferably Hawaiian red sea salt)
	Hot cooked rice, optional

1. Pierce pork with a fork; rub with liquid smoke and salt. Place pork in a 6-qt. slow cooker. Cook, covered, on low 8-10 hours or until pork is tender.
2. Remove roast; shred with 2 forks. Strain the cooking juices; skim fat. Return pork to slow cooker. Stir in enough cooking juices to moisten; heat through. If desired, serve with hot cooked rice.

Freeze option: Freeze cooled meat mixture and the juices in freezer containers. To use, partially thaw in refrigerator overnight. Heat through in a saucepan, stirring occasionally; add broth if necessary.

3 oz. cooked pork: 205 cal., 13g fat (5g sat. fat), 75mg chol., 504mg sod., 0 carb. (0 sugars, 0 fiber), 21g pro.
Diabetic exchanges: 3 medium-fat meat.

KALUA PORK

**HONEY-LIME
ROASTED CHICKEN**

HONEY-LIME
ROASTED CHICKEN

It's hard to believe this finger-licking main course starts with only five ingredients. The chicken is easy, light and so good. It's just as tasty prepared outside on the grill.

—Lori Carbonell, Springfield, VT

- -

Prep: 10 min.
Bake: 2½ hours + standing
Makes: 10 servings

1 **whole roasting chicken
(5 to 6 lbs.)**

½ **cup lime juice**
¼ **cup honey**
1 **Tbsp. stone-ground mustard
or spicy brown mustard**
1 **tsp. salt**
1 **tsp. ground cumin**

1. Preheat oven to 350°. Carefully loosen the skin from the entire chicken. Place breast side up on a rack in a roasting pan. In a small bowl, whisk the lime juice, honey, mustard, salt and cumin.

2. Using a turkey baster, baste under the chicken skin with ⅓ cup lime juice mixture. Tie drumsticks together.

Pour the remaining lime juice mixture over chicken.

3. Roast until a thermometer inserted in thickest part of thigh reads 170°-175°, 2-2½ hours. (Cover loosely with foil if chicken browns too quickly.) Let stand for 10 minutes before carving. If desired, remove and discard skin before serving.

4 oz. cooked chicken: 294 cal., 16g fat (4g sat. fat), 90mg chol., 354mg sod., 8g carb. (7g sugars, 0 fiber), 28g pro.

SHRIMP PASTA ALFREDO

SHRIMP PASTA ALFREDO

My son loves any recipe with Alfredo sauce. When he cooked as a bachelor, shrimp pasta was one of his first recipes. Now his children ask for it.

—Gail Lucas, Olive Branch, MS

- -

Takes: 25 min. • **Makes:** 4 servings

- 3 **cups uncooked bow tie pasta**
- 2 **cups frozen peas**
- 1 **lb. peeled and deveined cooked medium shrimp, tails removed**
- 1 **jar (15 oz.) Alfredo sauce**
- ¼ **cup shredded Parmesan cheese**

1. In a Dutch oven, cook the pasta according to package directions, adding peas during the last 3 minutes of cooking; drain and return to pan.

2. Stir in shrimp and sauce; heat through over medium heat, stirring occasionally. Sprinkle with cheese.

2 cups: 545 cal., 16g fat (9g sat. fat), 206mg chol., 750mg sod., 60g carb. (5g sugars, 6g fiber), 41g pro.

CHEESEBURGER & FRIES CASSEROLE

Kids love this casserole because it combines two of their favorite fast foods. And I like the fact that I can whip it up with just a few ingredients, and with almost no prep time.

—Karen Owen, Rising Sun, IN

- -

Prep: 10 min. • **Bake:** 50 min.
Makes: 8 servings

- 2 lbs. lean ground beef (90% lean)
- 1 can (10¾ oz.) condensed golden mushroom soup, undiluted
- 1 can (10¾ oz.) condensed cheddar cheese soup, undiluted
- 1 pkg. (20 oz.) frozen crinkle-cut french fries

1. Preheat oven to 350°. In a large skillet, cook beef over medium heat until no longer pink; drain. Stir in soups. Pour into a greased 13x9-in. baking dish.

2. Arrange french fries on top. Bake, uncovered, until the fries are golden brown, 50-55 minutes.

1½ cups: 352 cal., 17g fat (5g sat. fat), 62mg chol., 668mg sod., 25g carb. (1g sugars, 2g fiber), 25g pro.

CHEESEBURGER & FRIES CASSEROLE

TANGY BEEF TURNOVERS

BAKED HAM WITH PINEAPPLE

I first learned the technique for cooking ham with pineapple for a themed dinner that my husband and I hosted. Since it is widely known as the symbol of hospitality, pineapple was the star ingredient on our menu and on this lovely baked ham.
—JoAnn Fox, Johnson City, TN

- -

Prep: 10 min. • **Bake:** 2 hours
Makes: 20 servings

 1 fully cooked bone-in ham
    (6 to 8 lbs.)
    Whole cloves
 1 can (20 oz.) sliced pineapple
 ½ cup packed brown sugar
12 maraschino cherries

1. Place ham in roasting pan. Score the surface with shallow diagonal cuts, making diamond shapes; insert cloves into diamonds. Cover and bake at 325° for 1½ hours. Drain pineapple, reserving ¼ cup of the juice. Combine brown sugar and reserved pineapple juice; pour over ham. Arrange pineapple slices and cherries on ham.
2. Bake, uncovered, 30-45 minutes longer or until a thermometer reads 140° and the ham is heated through.
3 oz. cooked ham: 219 cal., 13g fat (5g sat. fat), 48mg chol., 924mg sod., 8g carb. (8g sugars, 0 fiber), 17g pro.

TANGY BEEF TURNOVERS

My mom's recipe for these flavorful pockets called for dough made from scratch, but I streamlined the prep by using refrigerated crescent rolls. My children love the turnovers plain or dipped in ketchup.
—Claudia Bodeker, Ash Flat, AR

- -

Takes: 30 min. • **Makes:** 1 dozen

 1 lb. ground beef
 1 medium onion, chopped
 1 jar (16 oz.) sauerkraut,
    rinsed, drained and chopped
 1 cup shredded Swiss cheese
 3 tubes (8 oz. each)
    refrigerated crescent rolls

1. In a large skillet, cook the beef and onion over medium heat until meat is no longer pink; drain. Add sauerkraut and cheese.
2. Unroll crescent roll dough and separate into rectangles. Place on greased baking sheets; pinch seams to seal. Place ½ cup beef mixture in the center of each rectangle. Bring corners to the center and pinch to seal. Bake at 375° for 15-18 minutes or until golden brown.
2 turnovers: 634 cal., 35g fat (7g sat. fat), 63mg chol., 1426mg sod., 54g carb. (14g sugars, 2g fiber), 27g pro.

**BAKED HAM
WITH PINEAPPLE**

COOKIES, BARS, BROWNIES & CANDIES

**MAPLE-BACON
WHITE CHOCOLATE
FUDGE P. 206**

1

2

3

4

5

THANKS TO THESE SIMPLE RECIPES, YOU CAN ALWAYS
HAVE A LITTLE SOMETHING SWEET ON HAND.

MAGIC BROWNIE BARS

One of my all-time favorite treats as a kid was magic cookie bars. This recipe combines the same classic flavors in a brownie!
—Mandy Rivers, Lexington, SC

- -

Prep: 15 min.
Bake: 35 min. + cooling
Makes: 3 dozen

- 1 pkg. (17½ oz.) brownie mix
- 1 pkg. (11 oz.) butterscotch chips
- 2 cups sweetened shredded coconut
- 1 cup chopped pecans, optional
- 1 can (14 oz.) sweetened condensed milk

1. Preheat the oven to 350°. Line a 13x9-in. baking pan with foil, letting ends extend up sides; grease the foil.
2. Prepare brownie mix batter according to package directions. Transfer to prepared pan. Top with butterscotch chips, coconut and, if desired, pecans. Drizzle with milk. Bake until topping is light golden, 35-40 minutes.
3. Cool completely in pan on a wire rack. Lifting with foil, remove the brownies from pan. Cut into bars. Store in an airtight container.
1 bar: 200 cal., 10g fat (5g sat. fat), 14mg chol., 91mg sod., 25g carb. (21g sugars, 1g fiber), 3g pro.

JELLY BEAN BARK

JELLY BEAN BARK

Homemade Easter candy really doesn't get easier than this. It's so simple—all you need are three ingredients, a microwave and a pan. It makes a perfect gift!
—Mavis Dement, Marcus, IA

- -

Prep: 15 min. + standing
Makes: 2 lbs.

- 1 Tbsp. butter
- 1¼ lbs. white candy coating, coarsely chopped
- 2 cups small jelly beans

1. Line a 15x10x1-in. pan with foil; grease foil with the butter. In a microwave, melt candy coating; stir until smooth. Spread into the prepared pan. Top with jelly beans, pressing to adhere. Let candy stand until set.
2. Cut or break bark into pieces. Store in an airtight container.
1 oz.: 154 cal., 5g fat (5g sat. fat), 1mg chol., 10mg sod., 27g carb. (23g sugars, 0 fiber), 0 pro.

SALTINE TOFFEE BARK

Everyone loves these salty-sweet treasures—their flavor is simply irresistible. The crunchy bark is like brittle, but better. Get ready for a new family favorite!
—Laura Cox, South Dennis, MA

- -

Prep: 15 min.
Bake: 10 min. + chilling
Makes: 2 lbs.

40	saltines
1	cup butter, cubed
¾	cup sugar
2	cups semisweet chocolate chips
1	pkg. (8 oz.) milk chocolate English toffee bits

1. Line a 15x10x1-in. baking pan with heavy-duty foil. Arrange saltines in a single layer on foil; set pan aside.
2. In a large, heavy saucepan over medium heat, melt butter. Stir in sugar. Bring to a boil; cook and stir for 1-2 minutes or until the sugar is dissolved. Pour evenly over crackers.
3. Bake at 350° for 8-10 minutes or until bubbly. Immediately sprinkle with chocolate chips. Allow chips to soften for a few minutes; spread them over top. Sprinkle with toffee bits. Cool.
4. Cover and refrigerate for 1 hour or until set. Break into pieces. Store in an airtight container.
1 oz.: 171 cal., 12g fat (7g sat. fat), 21mg chol., 119mg sod., 18g carb. (11g sugars, 1g fiber), 1g pro.

ORANGE CRISPIES

Add a splash of sunshine to your cookie jar with this recipe. When I want to spread cheer, I'll bake up a double batch to share.
—Ruth Gladstone, Brunswick, MD

- -

Prep: 15 min. • **Bake:** 10 min./batch
Makes: 3½ dozen

1	cup shortening
1	cup sugar
1	large egg, room temperature
1½	tsp. orange extract
½	tsp. salt
1½	cups all-purpose flour
	Optional: Sugar or orange-colored sugar

1. In a small bowl, cream shortening and sugar until mixture is light and fluffy, 5-7 minutes. Beat in the egg, extract and salt. Add the flour; mix well. Drop rounded tablespoons of dough 2 in. apart onto ungreased baking sheets.
2. Bake at 375° until edges begin to brown, about 10 minutes. Cool for 1-2 minutes; remove from pans to wire racks. If desired, sprinkle warm cookies with sugar.
1 cookie with sugar topping: 79 cal., 5g fat (1g sat. fat), 4mg chol., 30mg sod., 18g carb. (5g sugars, 0 fiber), 1g pro.

ORANGE CRISPIES

TIGER BUTTER FUDGE

TIGER BUTTER FUDGE

My younger brother and I share a passion for candymaking. We love this smooth and creamy fudge recipe from a co-worker of mine. It features the classic combination of peanut butter and chocolate.

—Peg Kipp, Lewisburg, PA

- -

Prep: 25 min. + chilling
Makes: 81 pieces

1½ tsp. butter
2⅔ cups vanilla or white chips
1 cup creamy peanut butter, divided
2 Tbsp. shortening, divided
2⅔ cups milk chocolate chips

1. Line a 9-in. square pan with foil and grease the foil with butter; set aside. In a heavy saucepan, melt vanilla chips, ½ cup peanut butter and 1 Tbsp. shortening over low heat; cook and stir constantly until smooth. Pour into prepared pan.

2. In another heavy saucepan, melt milk chocolate chips, ½ cup peanut butter and 1 Tbsp. shortening over low heat; cook and stir constantly until smooth. Drizzle over the vanilla layer. Swirl with a knife. Refrigerate for 30 minutes or until firm. Using the foil, lift fudge out of pan. Gently peel off foil; cut into 1-in. squares.

1 piece: 82 cal., 5g fat (3g sat. fat), 3mg chol., 23mg sod., 7g carb. (6g sugars, 0 fiber), 1g pro.

MAINE POTATO CANDY

MAINE POTATO CANDY

Years ago, folks in Maine ate potatoes every day— and wisely used up the leftovers in bread, doughnuts and candy.

—Barbara Allen, Chelmsford, MA

- -

Prep: 30 min. + chilling
Makes: 40 pieces

- 4 cups confectioners' sugar
- 4 cups sweetened shredded coconut
- ¾ cup cold mashed potatoes (without added milk and butter)
- 1½ tsp. vanilla extract
- ½ tsp. salt
- 1 lb. dark chocolate candy coating, coarsely chopped

1. In a large bowl, combine the first 5 ingredients. Line a 9-in. square pan with foil; butter the foil. Spread the coconut mixture into pan. Cover and chill overnight. Cut chilled mixture into 2x1-in. rectangles. Cover and freeze pieces.

2. In a microwave, melt the candy coating; stir until smooth. Dip bars in coating; allow excess to drip off. Place on waxed paper to set. Store in an airtight container.

1 piece: 155 cal., 7g fat (6g sat. fat), 0 chol., 55mg sod., 25g carb. (23g sugars, 1g fiber), 1g pro.

★ ★ ★ ★ ★ **READER REVIEW**

"Don't let the name or ingredients throw you off. If you like coconut, this is the one to make! It is so good. People are impressed by these homemade candies."

—BECKIHOMECKI, TASTEOFHOME.COM

POLKA-DOT MACAROONS

Macaroons studded with M&M's are very easy to mix up in a hurry. That's good, because—believe me—they never last long.

—Janice Lass, Dorr, MI

Prep: 15 min.
Bake: 10 min./batch + cooling
Makes: about 4½ dozen

- 5 **cups sweetened shredded coconut**
- 1 **can (14 oz.) sweetened condensed milk**
- ½ **cup all-purpose flour**
- 1½ **cups M&M's minis**

1. Preheat oven to 350°. In a large bowl, mix coconut, milk and flour until blended; stir in the M&M's.
2. Drop the mixture by rounded tablespoonfuls 2 in. apart onto greased baking sheets. Bake until the edges are lightly browned, 8-10 minutes or. Remove from pans to wire racks to cool.

Freeze option: Freeze cookies, layered between waxed paper, in freezer containers. To use, thaw before serving.

1 cookie: 99 cal., 5g fat (4g sat. fat), 3mg chol., 31mg sod., 13g carb. (10g sugars, 1g fiber), 1g pro.

POLKA-DOT MACAROONS

CHOCOLATY S'MORES BARS

SNICKERS COOKIES

Though you wouldn't know by looking at them, you'll find a sweet surprise inside these cookies! My mother got this recipe from a fellow teacher at her school. It's a great way to dress up refrigerated cookie dough. Yum!

—Kari Pease, Conconully, WA

Takes: 30 min. • **Makes:** 2 dozen

- 1 tube refrigerated chocolate chip cookie dough
- 24 miniature Snickers candy bars

Preheat oven to 350°. Cut dough into ¼-in.-thick slices. Place a candy bar on each slice and wrap dough around it. Place 2 in. apart on ungreased baking sheets. Bake until lightly browned, 8-10 minutes. Remove to wire racks to cool.

1 cookie: 123 cal., 5g fat (2g sat. fat), 6mg chol., 59mg sod., 17g carb. (4g sugars, 0 fiber), 2g pro.

TEST KITCHEN TIP
Have fun with this quick, easy recipe by substituting all kinds of chocolate bars. Try using Mounds, Heath, Milky Way, Mr. Goodbar, or even Butterfinger bars.

CHOCOLATY S'MORES BARS

One night, my husband had some friends over to play poker and he requested these s'mores bars. The players polished off the pan and asked for more! I shared the recipe and now their families make them, too.

—Rebecca Shipp, Beebe, AR

Prep: 15 min. + cooling
Makes: 1½ dozen

- ¼ cup butter, cubed
- 1 pkg. (10 oz.) large marshmallows
- 1 pkg. (12 oz.) Golden Grahams cereal
- ⅓ cup milk chocolate chips, melted

1. In a large saucepan, melt butter over low heat. Add marshmallows; cook and stir until blended. Remove from heat. Stir in cereal until coated.
2. Press into a greased 13x9-in. pan using a buttered spatula. Drizzle with melted chocolate. Cool completely before cutting. Store the bars in an airtight container.

1 bar: 159 cal., 4g fat (2g sat. fat), 7mg chol., 197mg sod., 30g carb. (17g sugars, 1g fiber), 1g pro.

SNICKERS
COOKIES

CHERRY CRUMB DESSERT BARS

CHERRY CRUMB DESSERT BARS

This sweet treat is especially good with a dollop of whipped cream or a scoop of ice cream. The crumbly topping adds a wonderful nutty flavor, and nobody will guess this streusel started with a handy cake mix!

—Ann Eastman, Santa Monica, CA

- -

Prep: 15 min. • **Bake:** 30 min.
Makes: 16 servings

½ cup cold butter
1 pkg. yellow cake mix (regular size)
1 can (21 oz.) cherry or blueberry pie filling
½ cup chopped walnuts

1. In a large bowl, cut butter into cake mix until crumbly. Set aside 1 cup for topping. Pat remaining crumbs onto the bottom and ½ in. up the sides of a greased 13x9-in. baking pan.
2. Spread pie filling over crust. Combine the walnuts with reserved crumbs; sprinkle over top. Bake at 350° for 30-35 minutes or until golden brown. Cut into bars.

1 piece: 294 cal., 11g fat (5g sat. fat), 15mg chol., 290mg sod., 46g carb. (26g sugars, 2g fiber), 3g pro.

PEANUT BUTTER CORNFLAKE BARS

Peanut butter cornflake bars were one of my favorite treats when I was a little girl. They are very versatile. A friend likes to spread a cup of chocolate chips , melted, over the top. Be sure to let the chocolate set before cutting into these simply delicious bars.

—Laura Campbell, Lisbon, ME

- -

Prep/Cook time: 15 min. + standing
Makes: 20 servings

1½ **cups creamy peanut butter**
 1 **cup sugar**
 1 **cup light corn syrup**
 6 **cups cornflakes**

In a large saucepan, combine peanut butter, sugar and corn syrup. Cook and stir over medium-low heat until sugar is dissolved. Remove from the heat; stir in cereal. Spread mixture into a greased 13x9-in. pan; press lightly. Let stand until set, about 1 hour.

1 bar: 234 cal., 10g fat (2g sat. fat), 0 chol., 154mg sod., 35g carb. (26g sugars, 1g fiber), 5g pro.

PEANUT BUTTER CORNFLAKE BARS

FROZEN SANDWICH COOKIES

It takes only three ingredients to make these chilled sandwich cookies. You'll love the pretty pink filling.

—Mary Ann Irvine, Lombard, IL

- -

Prep: 10 min. + freezing
Makes: 8 sandwich cookies

 ½ **cup spreadable strawberry cream cheese**
 ¼ **cup strawberry yogurt**
16 **chocolate wafers**

In a small bowl, beat cream cheese and yogurt until blended. Spread on bottoms of half of the chocolate wafers; top with remaining wafers. Place on a baking sheet. Freeze for 30 minutes or until firm. Serve cookies immediately or wrap in foil and return to freezer for later.

1 sandwich cookie: 110 cal., 6g fat (4g sat. fat), 13mg chol., 124mg sod., 13g carb. (4g sugars, 0 fiber), 2g pro.
Frozen Blueberry Sandwich Cookies: Use blueberry spreadable cream cheese and yogurt instead of the strawberry varieties.

PEANUT BUTTER CHOCOLATE BARS

These chewy peanut butter chocolate bars are the perfect no-fuss addition to a potluck or bake sale. The trick is to get them into the refrigerator before they all disappear!

—Lorri Speer, Centralia, WA

- -

Prep: 30 min. + chilling
Makes: 2 dozen

- 1 **cup sugar**
- 1 **cup light corn syrup**
- 1 **cup peanut butter**
- 6 **cups crisp rice cereal**
- 2 **cups semisweet chocolate chips, melted**

In a large saucepan, combine sugar, corn syrup and peanut butter. Cook and stir over medium-low heat until sugar is dissolved. Remove from the heat; stir in the cereal. Spread into a greased 13x9-in. pan; press lightly. Spread melted chocolate over top; refrigerate until set. Cut into bars.

1 bar: 302 cal., 14g fat (6g sat. fat), 0 chol., 96mg sod., 46g carb. (37g sugars, 2g fiber), 4g pro.

TEST KITCHEN TIP
Corn syrup is an invert sugar, meaning it is liquid in its natural state. This quality helps it stop sugar crystals from forming in frostings, candies and other sweet recipes.

PEANUT BUTTER CHOCOLATE BARS

CHOCOLATE-CARAMEL TRUFFLES

CHOCOLATE-CARAMEL TRUFFLES

These candies disappear as fast as I can make them. The five-ingredient microwave recipe is easy and fun to make. And when drizzled with white chocolate and packaged with ribbon, they're a pretty gift.

—Charlotte Midthun, Granite Falls, MN

- -

Prep: 1 hour + chilling
Makes: 2½ dozen

- 26 **caramels**
- 1 **cup milk chocolate chips**
- ¼ **cup heavy whipping cream**
- 1⅓ **cups semisweet chocolate chips**
- 1 **Tbsp. shortening**

1. Line an 8-in. square pan with foil; set aside. In a microwave-safe bowl, combine caramels, milk chocolate and cream. Microwave, uncovered, on high for 1 minute; stir. Microwave 1 minute longer, stirring mixture every 15 seconds or until caramels are melted and mixture is smooth. Spread into the prepared pan and refrigerate for 1 hour or until firm.

2. Using the foil, lift candy out of pan. Cut into 30 pieces and roll each piece into a 1-in. ball. Cover and refrigerate for 1 hour or until firm.

3. In a microwave-safe bowl, melt semisweet chips and shortening; stir until smooth. Dip caramels in chocolate; allow excess to drip off. Place on waxed paper; let stand until set. If desired, use additional melted chocolate to drizzle over truffles. Refrigerate until firm.

1 truffle: 110 cal., 6g fat (3g sat. fat), 4mg chol., 27mg sod., 15g carb. (13g sugars, 1g fiber), 1g pro.

RASPBERRY
ALMOND STRIPS

RASPBERRY ALMOND STRIPS

A cup of tea is the perfect complement to these simple, scrumptious cookie strips dressed up with raspberry filling. Chopped almonds make them an extra-special treat.
—*Taste of Home* Test Kitchen

- -

Prep: 20 min. • **Bake:** 15 min./batch
Makes: 32 cookies

- 1 tube (16½ oz.) refrigerated sugar cookie dough, softened
- ⅔ cup all-purpose flour
- ½ cup finely chopped almonds
- 6 Tbsp. raspberry cake and pastry filling

1. Preheat oven to 350°. In a large bowl, beat the cookie dough, flour and almonds until blended. Divide dough in half. Roll each half into a 13½x2-in. rectangle on an ungreased baking sheet.
2. Using a wooden spoon handle, make a ¼-in.-deep indentation lengthwise down the center of each rectangle. Bake 5 minutes.
3. Spoon raspberry filling into indentation. Bake 8-10 minutes longer or until cookie is golden brown. Cool on pans 2 minutes.
4. Remove from pans to a cutting board; cut each rectangle crosswise into 16 slices. Transfer to wire racks to cool.

1 cookie: 106 cal., 4g fat (1g sat. fat), 2mg chol., 55mg sod., 16g carb. (9g sugars, 1g fiber), 1g pro.

LEMON CRISP COOKIES

LEMON CRISP COOKIES

Here's a quick-to-fix delight that's perfect to make when you've forgotten a treat for a bake sale or potluck. They take only 10 minutes to whip up! The sunny yellow color, big lemon flavor and delightful crunch are sure to bring smiles.
—Julia Livingston, Frostproof, FL

- -

Takes: 30 min.
Makes: about 4 dozen

- 1 pkg. lemon cake mix (regular size)
- 1 cup crisp rice cereal
- ½ cup butter, melted
- 1 large egg, room temperature, lightly beaten
- 1 tsp. grated lemon zest

1. Preheat oven to 350°. In a large bowl, combine all the ingredients (dough will be crumbly). Shape into 1-in. balls. Place balls 2 in. apart on ungreased baking sheets.
2. Bake 10-12 minutes or until set. Cool 1 minute; remove from pan to a wire rack to cool completely.

1 cookie: 61 cal., 2g fat (2g sat. fat), 9mg chol., 100mg sod., 10g carb. (15g sugars, 0 fiber), 0g pro.

QUICK COCONUT MACAROONS

Chewy, simple and so good, these bite-sized cookies are perfect for bake sales, that is, if your family doesn't devour them first!

—Sabrina Shafer, Minooka, IL

Takes: 25 min. • **Makes:** 1½ dozen

- 2½ **cups sweetened shredded coconut**
- ⅓ **cup all-purpose flour**
- ⅛ **tsp. salt**
- ⅔ **cup sweetened condensed milk**
- 1 **tsp. vanilla extract**

1. Preheat oven to 350°. In a small bowl, combine the coconut, flour and salt. Add milk and vanilla; mix well (batter will be stiff).

2. Drop by tablespoonfuls 1 in. apart onto a greased baking sheet. Bake 15-20 minutes or until golden brown. Remove to wire racks.

1 cookie: 110 cal., 6g fat (5g sat. fat), 4mg chol., 65mg sod., 14g carb. (11g sugars, 1g fiber), 2g pro.

MAPLE-BACON WHITE CHOCOLATE FUDGE

Bored with the same old fudge? Prepare it with white chips, add maple flavoring and load it up with bacon. Then be prepared to share the recipe.

—Mindie Hilton, Susanville, CA

Prep: 10 min. + chilling
Makes: 81 pieces

- 1 **tsp. plus ¼ cup butter, cubed, divided**
- 10 **slices ready-to-serve fully cooked bacon**
- 2 **pkg. (10 to 12 oz. each) white baking chips**
- 1 **can (14 oz.) sweetened condensed milk**
- ¾ **tsp. maple flavoring**

1. Line a 9-in. square pan with foil; grease foil with 1 tsp. butter. Heat bacon according to the package directions. Crumble the bacon and set aside.

2. In a large microwave-safe bowl, combine baking chips, condensed milk, flavoring and remaining butter. Microwave on high 1 minute; stir until smooth. (If the chips aren't completely melted, microwave in 10- to 20-second intervals until melted; stir until smooth.) Stir in the bacon; pour into prepared pan. Refrigerate fudge, covered, 2 hours or until firm.

3. Using foil, lift fudge out of pan. Gently remove the foil; cut fudge into 1-in. squares.

To make ahead: Store fudge, layered between waxed paper, in an airtight container in the refrigerator. Serve at room temperature.

Freeze option: Wrap fudge in waxed paper, then in foil. Place in freezer containers and freeze. To use, bring wrapped fudge to room temperature.

1 piece: 62 cal., 4g fat (2g sat. fat), 5mg chol., 26mg sod., 7g carb. (7g sugars, 0 fiber), 1g pro.

MAPLE-BACON WHITE CHOCOLATE FUDGE

TOFFEE TURTLE SQUARES

TOFFEE TURTLE SQUARES

Here's an easy way to make turtle candy for a big group. These bars are very rich, so a little square will do ya.

—Glenna Tooman, Boise, ID

- -

Prep: 15 min.
Bake: 15 min. + cooling
Makes: 4 dozen

- 2 **cups all-purpose flour**
- 1½ **cups packed brown sugar, divided**
- 1 **cup plus 3 Tbsp. softened butter, divided**
- 1½ **cups coarsely chopped pecans**
- 1½ **cups semisweet chocolate chips**

1. Preheat the oven to 350°. Line a 13x9-in. baking pan with parchment, letting the ends extend up the sides.

2. Beat flour, 1 cup brown sugar and ½ cup butter until well blended (mixture will be dry and crumbly). Firmly press into prepared pan. Sprinkle pecans over flour mixture.

3. In a small saucepan, combine the remaining brown sugar and remaining butter. Bring to a boil over medium heat. Boil until sugar is dissolved, stirring constantly, about 1 minute. Carefully pour mixture over pecans. Bake until bubbly and edges start to brown, 15-20 minutes.

4. Remove from oven. Immediately sprinkle with chocolate chips. Let stand until chocolate begins to melt; spread evenly. Cool completely in pan on a wire rack. Lifting with parchment, remove from pan. Cut into squares.

1 bar: 134 cal., 9g fat (4g sat. fat), 12mg chol., 39mg sod., 15g carb. (10g sugars, 1g fiber), 1g pro.

PEANUT BUTTER CANDY

PEANUT BUTTER CANDY

During the holidays, I make lots of candy for friends, and this simple recipe seems to be a favorite. The white chocolate and chunky peanut butter make a perfect blend.

—Deloris Morrow, Lake City, IA

- -

Prep: 10 min. + cooling
Makes: 16 pieces.

½ tsp. butter
1¼ lbs. white candy coating, coarsely chopped
1½ cups chunky peanut butter

1. Line a 9-in. square pan with foil; butter the foil and set aside.
2. In a microwave-safe bowl, melt candy coating; stir until smooth. Stir in the peanut butter until melted. Transfer to prepared pan. Cool to room temperature. Cut into squares.

1 piece: 331 cal., 22g fat (11g sat. fat), 0 chol., 118mg sod., 30g carb. (26g sugars, 2g fiber), 6g pro.

POTATO CHIP BITES

A friend at church gave me the recipe for these buttery, light and crisp cookies. It has never failed to bring me compliments.
—Brenda Stone, Sterrett, AL

Prep: 15 min. + chilling
Bake: 10 min./per batch + cooling
Makes: about 3 dozen

  2 cups butter, softened
1¼ cups sugar
  3 tsp. vanilla extract
3½ cups all-purpose flour
2⅓ cups crushed potato chips
     Optional: 2 cups semisweet
     chocolate chips, additional
     crushed potato chips

1. In a large bowl, cream butter and sugar until light and fluffy, 5-7 minutes. Beat in vanilla. In another bowl, whisk flour and crushed chips; gradually beat into creamed mixture.
2. Divide dough in half; shape each into a 10-in.-long roll. Wrap and refrigerate 1 hour or until firm.
3. Preheat oven to 350°. Unwrap and cut dough crosswise into ½-in. slices. Place 1 in. apart on ungreased baking sheets. Bake 10-12 minutes or until bottoms are light brown. Cool on pans 2 minutes. Remove to wire racks to cool completely. If desired, melt the chocolate chips; dip each cookie halfway into chocolate; allow excess to drip off. Place on waxed paper. If desired, sprinkle with additional crushed potato chips.
1 cookie: 164 cal., 10g fat (6g sat. fat), 24mg chol., 93mg sod., 16g carb. (6g sugars, 0 fiber), 1g pro.

**POTATO CHIP
BITES**

MICROWAVE OATMEAL BARS

LEMON SNOWFLAKES

You'll need just four ingredients to make these delightful cookies. Confectioners' sugar highlights the cracked tops to give them their snowflake appearance.

—Linda Barry, Dianna, TX

- -

Prep: 30 min. • **Bake:** 10 min./batch
Makes: 5½ dozen

- 1 pkg. lemon cake mix (regular size)
- 2¼ cups whipped topping
- 1 large egg, room temperature
   Confectioners' sugar

1. In a large bowl, combine cake mix, whipped topping and egg until well blended. Batter will be very sticky.
2. Drop by teaspoonfuls into the confectioners' sugar; roll lightly to coat. Place cookies on ungreased baking sheets. Bake at 350° for 10-12 minutes or until lightly browned and tops are cracked. Remove to wire racks to cool.
1 cookie: 37 cal., 1g fat (1g sat. fat), 3mg chol., 59mg sod., 7g carb. (4g sugars, 0 fiber), 0 pro.

MICROWAVE OATMEAL BARS

My mother shared this speedy recipe with me. There are not a lot of ingredients, and these microwave treats are easy enough for kids to prepare.
—Annette Self, Junction City, OH

- -

Prep: 20 min. + chilling
Makes: 15 servings

- 2 cups quick-cooking oats
- ½ cup packed brown sugar
- ½ cup butter, melted
- ¼ cup corn syrup
- 1 cup semisweet chocolate chips

1. In a large bowl, combine the oats and brown sugar. Stir in butter and corn syrup. Press into a greased 9-in. square microwave-safe dish.
2. Microwave, uncovered, on high for 1½ minutes. Rotate a half turn; microwave 1½ minutes longer. Sprinkle with the chocolate chips. Microwave at 30% power for about 4½ minutes or until chips are glossy; spread chocolate evenly over top.
3. Refrigerate for 15-20 minutes before cutting.
1 piece: 192 cal., 10g fat (6g sat. fat), 16mg chol., 56mg sod., 26g carb. (18g sugars, 2g fiber), 2g pro.

LEMON
SNOWFLAKES

HOMEMADE
HOLIDAY
MARSHMALLOWS

HOMEMADE HOLIDAY MARSHMALLOWS

This recipe was my grandpa's favorite. Every Christmas, he would busy himself by making marshmallows for his family and friends.

—Diana Byron, New London, OH

- -

Prep: 55 min. + standing
Makes: about 9½ dozen

- 2   **tsp. butter**
- 3   **envelopes unflavored gelatin**
- 1   **cup cold water, divided**
- 2   **cups sugar**
- 1   **cup light corn syrup**
- ⅛   **tsp. salt**
- 1   **tsp. clear vanilla extract**

Optional toppings: Melted chocolate, hot fudge and/or caramel ice cream topping
Optional garnishes: Baking cocoa, confectioners' sugar, crushed assorted candies, chopped nuts, colored sugars and/or sprinkles

1. Line a 13x9-in. pan with foil and grease the foil with butter; set aside.
2. In a large metal bowl, sprinkle the gelatin over ½ cup water; set aside. In a large heavy saucepan, combine sugar, corn syrup, salt and remaining water. Bring mixture to a boil, stirring occasionally. Cook, without stirring, until a candy thermometer reads 240° (soft-ball stage).
3. Remove from heat and gradually add to gelatin. Beat on high speed until mixture is thick and the volume is doubled, about 15 minutes. Beat in vanilla. Spread into the prepared pan. Cover and let stand at room temperature 6 hours or overnight.
4. Using foil, lift the marshmallows out of pan. With a knife or pizza cutter coated with cooking spray, cut into 1-in. squares. Dip or drizzle marshmallows with toppings if desired; coat with the garnishes as desired. Store in an airtight container in a cool, dry place.

1 plain marshmallow: 22 cal., 0 fat (0 sat. fat), 0 chol., 5mg sod., 6g carb. (4g sugars, 0 fiber), 0 pro.

VANILLA MERINGUE COOKIES

These sweet little swirls are light as can be. They're all you need after a rich, special dinner.

—Jenni Sharp, Milwaukee, WI

- -

Prep: 20 min.
Bake: 40 min. + standing
Makes: about 5 dozen

  3 **large egg whites**
1½ **tsp. clear or regular vanilla extract**
 ¼ **tsp. cream of tartar**
    Dash salt
 ⅔ **cup sugar**

1. Place the egg whites in a small bowl; let stand at room temperature 30 minutes.

2. Preheat oven to 250°. Add the vanilla, cream of tartar and salt to egg whites; beat on medium speed until foamy. Gradually add sugar, 1 Tbsp. at a time, beating on high after each addition, until the sugar is dissolved. Continue beating until stiff glossy peaks form, about 7 minutes.

3. Cut a small hole in the tip of a pastry bag or in a corner of a food-safe bag; insert a #32 star tip. Transfer meringue to bag. Pipe 1¼-in.-diameter cookies 2 in. apart onto parchment-lined baking sheets.

4. Bake cookies until they are firm to the touch, 40-45 minutes. Turn off oven; leave meringues in oven 1 hour (leave oven door closed). Remove from the oven; cool completely on baking sheets. Remove meringues from paper; store in an airtight container at room temperature.

1 cookie: 10 cal., 0 fat (0 sat. fat), 0 chol., 5mg sod., 2g carb. (2g sugars, 0 fiber), 0 pro. **Diabetic exchanges:** 1 free food.

PEANUT BUTTER COOKIE CUPS

I'm a busy schoolteacher and pastor's wife and I wouldn't dare show my face at a church dinner or bake sale without some of these tempting peanut butter treats. They're quick and easy to make and always a hit.

—Kristi Tackett, Banner, KY

- -

Prep: 35 min. • **Bake:** 15 min.
Makes: 3 dozen

  1 **pkg. (17½ oz.) peanut butter cookie mix**
36 **miniature peanut butter cups, unwrapped**

1. Preheat oven to 350°. Prepare cookie mix according to package directions. Roll dough into thirty-six 1-in. balls. Place in greased miniature muffin cups. Press dough evenly onto bottom and up sides of each cup.

2. Bake 11-13 minutes or until set. Immediately place a peanut butter cup in each cookie cup; press down gently. Cool 10 minutes; carefully remove from pans.

1 cookie: 119 cal., 7g fat (2g sat. fat), 6mg chol., 89mg sod., 13g carb. (3g sugars, 1g fiber), 2g pro

VANILLA MERINGUE COOKIES

MINI BROWNIE TREATS

MINI BROWNIE TREATS

I like to take these quick and easy brownies to potlucks and family events. They are always snapped up in a flash!
—Pam Kokes, North Loup, NE

- -

Prep: 15 min.
Bake: 20 min. + cooling
Makes: 4 dozen

1	**pkg. fudge brownie mix** (13 x 9-in. pan size)
48	**striped or milk chocolate kisses**

1. Prepare brownie mix according to package directions for fudgelike brownies. Fill 48 paper-lined mini muffin cups two-thirds full of batter.
2. Bake at 350° for 18-21 minutes or until a toothpick inserted in the center comes out clean.
3. Immediately top each cup with a chocolate kiss. Cool for 10 minutes before removing from pans to wire racks to cool completely.

1 brownie: 94 cal., 5g fat (1g sat. fat), 9mg chol., 52mg sod., 12g carb. (8g sugars, 0 fiber), 1g pro.

**BIRTHDAY CAKE
FUDGE**

BIRTHDAY CAKE FUDGE

This decadent treat is the perfect sweet to make your birthday special. Or prepare it ahead and package it as a surprise gift for a friend.

—Rashanda Cobbins, Milwaukee, WI

Prep: 10 min. + chilling
Makes: 64 pieces

1	**can (14 oz.) sweetened condensed milk**
1½	**cups white baking chips**
3	**Tbsp. butter**
⅛	**tsp. salt**
1½	**cups unprepared Funfetti cake mix**
3	**Tbsp. sprinkles**

1. Line an 8-in. square pan with foil or parchment; grease foil lightly. In a large, heavy saucepan, cook and stir milk, baking chips, butter and salt over low heat until smooth. Remove from heat; stir in the cake mix until dissolved. Spread into prepared pan; top with sprinkles. Refrigerate fudge, covered, until firm, about 2 hours.

2. Using foil, lift fudge out of pan. Remove foil; cut fudge into 1-in. squares. Store candy in an airtight container in the refrigerator.

1 piece: 59 cal., 2g fat (2g sat. fat), 4mg chol., 47mg sod., 9g carb. (7g sugars, 0 fiber), 1g pro.

TEST KITCHEN TIP
Because the hallmark of great fudge is a smooth, velvety texture, be sure the cake mix used in this fudge is completely dissolved before moving on to the next step.

**EASY
SANDWICH
COOKIES**

EASY SANDWICH COOKIES

Colorful and cute, these cookies are extremely fast to make and disappear just as quickly from a cookie tray. Use sprinkles for some holiday flare.

—Darcie Cross, Novi, MI

Takes: 20 min.
Makes: 50-55 cookies

- 6 oz. white or milk chocolate candy coating, coarsely chopped
- 50 to 55 Oreo cookies
  Sprinkles

In a microwave, melt 2 oz. of candy coating, stirring until smooth. Spread over tops of a third of the cookies; decorate as desired with sprinkles. Place on waxed paper until set. Repeat with remaining cookies, coating and toppings.

1 cookie: 65 cal., 3g fat (1g sat. fat), 0 chol., 67mg sod., 9g carb. (6g sugars, 0 fiber), 1g pro.

★ ★ ★ ★ ★ **READER REVIEW**

"What a cute idea! Quick and simple, yet very fun! And who doesn't like Oreos?"

—MANUAHS, TASTEOFHOME.COM

SOUTH DAKOTA FRITO TREATS

SOUTH DAKOTA FRITO TREATS

Yep, they're made with corn chips, but don't let that fool you. These salty sweets were a staple after meetings at the quilt guild I once belonged to.

—Carol Tramp, Wynot, NE

Prep: 15 min. + standing
Makes: 2 dozen

- 2 pkg. (9¾ oz. each) corn chips, divided
- 2 cups semisweet chocolate chips, divided
- 1 cup sugar
- 1 cup light corn syrup
- 1 cup creamy peanut butter

1. Spread 1 pkg. corn chips on the bottom of a greased 13x9-in. baking pan; sprinkle 1 cup chocolate chips over the top.

2. In a large heavy saucepan, combine sugar and corn syrup. Bring to a boil; cook and stir 1 minute. Remove from heat; stir in peanut butter. Pour half of the peanut butter mixture over chip mixture. Top with remaining corn chips and chocolate chips; drizzle with remaining peanut butter mixture. Let stand until set. Cut into bars.

1 bar: 337 cal., 18g fat (5g sat. fat), 0 chol., 196mg sod., 43g carb. (29g sugars, 2g fiber), 5g pro.

CAKES, PIES & OTHER DESSERTS

1

RAINBOW SHERBET ANGEL FOOD CAKE P. 220

2

3

4

5

GOOD TIMES ARE MADE SWEETER WHEN YOU
SERVE UP ONE OF THESE SO-EASY SPECIALTIES.

FIVE-MINUTE BLUEBERRY PIE

RAINBOW SHERBET ANGEL FOOD CAKE

Talk about a dessert that pops off the plate! Sometimes I make this cake even more eye-catching by tinting the whipped cream. Use whatever sherbet flavor combination you like.

—Bonnie Hawkins, Elkhorn, WI

- -

Prep: 25 min. + freezing
Makes: 12 servings

- 1 prepared angel food cake (8 to 10 oz.)
- 3 cups rainbow sherbet, softened if necessary

WHIPPED CREAM

- 2 cups heavy whipping cream
- ⅓ cup confectioners' sugar
- 1 tsp. vanilla extract

1. Using a long serrated knife, cut cake horizontally into 4 layers. Place the bottom layer on a freezer-safe serving plate; spread cake with 1 cup sherbet. Repeat twice with middle cake layers and the remaining 2 cups sherbet. Top with the remaining cake layer. Freeze, covered, until sherbet is firm, about 1 hour.

2. In a large bowl, beat cream until it begins to thicken. Add confectioners' sugar and vanilla extract; beat until soft peaks form. Frost top and sides of cake. Freeze until firm.

3. Thaw in refrigerator 30 minutes before serving. Cut the cake with a serrated knife.

1 piece: 253 cal., 16g fat (10g sat. fat), 54mg chol., 174mg sod., 27g carb. (12g sugars, 2g fiber), 2g pro.

FIVE-MINUTE BLUEBERRY PIE

If you like the taste of fresh blueberries, you'll love this pie. Since it's a breeze to whip up, I make it often, especially in summer.

—Milda Anderson, Osceola, WI

- -

Prep: 15 min. + chilling
Makes: 8 servings

- ½ cup sugar
- 2 Tbsp. cornstarch
- ¾ cup water
- 4 cups fresh or frozen blueberries, thawed
- 1 graham cracker crust (9 in.)
  Whipped cream, optional

In a large saucepan, combine sugar and cornstarch. Stir in the water until smooth. Bring to a boil over medium heat; cook and stir for 2 minutes. Add blueberries. Cook for 3 minutes, stirring occasionally. Pour into crust. Chill. Garnish with whipped cream if desired.

1 piece: 202 cal., 6g fat (1g sat. fat), 0 chol., 122mg sod., 39g carb. (29g sugars, 2g fiber), 1g pro.

**RAINBOW SHERBET
ANGEL FOOD CAKE**

CHERRY PIE CHIMIS

In New Mexico, we love making these yummy fried pies for dessert. Because they just call for flour tortillas and canned pie filling, they're a snap to put together when time is short.
—Terry Ann Dominguez, Silver City, NM

- -

Takes: 25 min. • **Makes:** 6 servings

- 2 **cans (21 oz. each) cherry pie filling**
- 6 **flour tortillas (10 in.)**
  Oil for deep-fat frying
  Confectioners' sugar

1. Spoon pie filling down the center of each tortilla; fold sides and ends over the filling and roll up. Secure with toothpicks.

2. In an electric skillet or deep fryer, heat oil to 375°. Fry chimichangas, a few at a time, for 2 minutes on each side or until golden brown on both sides. Drain on paper towels, then dust with confectioners' sugar. Serve immediately.

1 chimi: 686 cal., 32g fat (3g sat. fat), 0 chol., 429mg sod., 87g carb. (48g sugars, 7g fiber), 7g pro.

Peach Pie Chimis: Substitute peach pie filling for cherry.

Caramel Apple Chimis: Substitute caramel apple pie filling for cherry. Dust with cinnamon and confectioners' sugar.

APPLE PIE A LA MODE

I was planning a dinner party, and wanted a dessert that wowed. My caramel apple ice cream pie certainly did the trick! Now it's a family favorite.
—Trisha Kruse, Eagle, ID

- -

Prep: 15 min. + freezing
Makes: 8 servings

- 1 **can (21 oz.) apple pie filling**
- 1 **graham cracker crust (9 in.)**
- 2 **cups butter pecan ice cream, softened if necessary**
- 1 **jar (12 oz.) hot caramel ice cream topping**
- ¼ **cup chopped pecans, toasted**

1. Spread half of the pie filling over crust. Top with half of the ice cream; freeze 30 minutes. Drizzle with half of the caramel topping; layer with the remaining pie filling. Freeze pie 30 minutes. Scoop the remaining ice cream over top. Freeze, covered, until firm.

2. Remove from freezer 30 minutes before serving. In a microwave, warm remaining caramel topping. Serve pie with the warm caramel topping; sprinkle with pecans.

Note: To toast nuts, bake in a shallow pan in a 350° oven for 5-10 minutes or cook in a skillet over low heat until lightly browned, stirring occasionally.

1 piece: 398 cal., 14g fat (4g sat. fat), 13mg chol., 357mg sod., 69g carb. (59g sugars, 2g fiber), 3g pro.

APPLE PIE A LA MODE

SONORAN SUNSET WATERMELON ICE

If you didn't think watermelon and cilantro could go together, this recipe will be a pleasant surprise! Sprinkle pomegranate seeds and a sprig of cilantro on top for extra flair.

—Jeanne Holt, St. Paul, MN

- -

Prep: 15 min. + cooling
Process: 10 min. + freezing
Makes: 6 servings

½ cup sugar
¼ cup water
4 cups cubed seedless watermelon
3 Tbsp. lime juice
2 Tbsp. pomegranate juice
1 Tbsp. minced fresh cilantro
Dash salt

1. In a small saucepan, bring the sugar and water to a boil; cook and stir until the sugar is dissolved. Cool completely.

2. Puree watermelon in a blender. Transfer to a large bowl; stir in sugar syrup and the remaining ingredients. Refrigerate until cold.

3. Pour watermelon mixture into cylinder of ice cream maker; freeze according to the manufacturer's directions. Transfer to freezer containers, allowing headspace for expansion. Freeze 4 hours or until firm.

½ cup: 100 cal., 0 fat (0 sat. fat), 0 chol., 246mg sod., 26g carb. (24g sugars, 0 fiber), 1g pro. **Diabetic exchanges:** 1½ starch, ½ fruit.

STRAWBERRY CAKE

STRAWBERRY CAKE

Garnish the top of the cake with fresh strawberries to hint at the flavor of this pretty pink treat before you cut it—or let it be a surprise!

—Pam Anderson, Billings, MT

- -

Prep: 25 min.
Bake: 25 min. + cooling
Makes: 16 servings

1	**pkg. white cake mix (regular size)**
1	**pkg. (3 oz.) strawberry gelatin**
1	**cup water**
½	**cup canola oil**
4	**large egg whites, room temperature**
½	**cup mashed unsweetened strawberries**
	Whipped cream or frosting of your choice

1. Preheat oven to 350°. In a large bowl, combine dry cake mix, gelatin powder, water and oil. Beat on low speed 1 minute or until moistened; beat on medium 4 minutes.

2. In a small bowl with clean beaters, beat egg whites on high speed until stiff peaks form. Fold egg whites and mashed strawberries into the cake batter.

3. Pour into 3 greased and floured 8-in. round baking pans. Bake 25-30 minutes or until a toothpick comes out clean. Cool 10 minutes before removing from pans to wire racks to cool completely.

4. Spread whipped cream or frosting between layers and over the top and sides of cake. If frosted with whipped cream, store in the refrigerator.

1 piece: 222 cal., 10g fat (2g sat. fat), 0 chol., 231mg sod., 31g carb. (19g sugars, 1g fiber), 3g pro.

BERRY ICE MILK POPS

Nothing says summer like an ice pop. Kids and adults alike love this fruit-filled version.

—Sharon Guinta, Stamford, CT

- -

Prep: 10 min. + freezing
Makes: 10 pops

1¾ cups 2% milk, divided
1 to 2 Tbsp. honey
¼ tsp. vanilla extract
1½ cups fresh raspberries
1 cup fresh blueberries
10 freezer pop molds or
    10 paper cups (3 oz. each)
    and wooden pop sticks

1. In a microwave, warm ¼ cup milk; stir in honey until blended. Stir in the remaining 1½ cups milk and vanilla.
2. Divide berries among molds; cover with the milk mixture. Top the molds with holders. If using cups, top with foil and insert sticks through foil. Freeze until firm.

1 pop: 51 cal., 2g fat (1g sat. fat), 4mg chol., 19mg sod., 8g carb. (6g sugars, 2g fiber), 2g pro.
Diabetic exchanges: ½ starch.

TEST KITCHEN TIP
For easy cleanup, spritz the measuring spoon with cooking spray before measuring sticky ingredients like honey.

BERRY ICE MILK POPS

BLOOD ORANGE CARAMEL TARTE TATIN

BLOOD ORANGE CARAMEL TARTE TATIN

I had never had blood oranges until moving to California. The season is short, so I use them in everything while I can get them. That sweet orange flavor with some brown sugar is a perfect combination. Whenever I have something to go to, my friends demand I bring this dessert!
—Pamela Butkowski, Hermosa Beach, CA

- -

Prep: 20 min.
Bake: 20 min. + cooling
Makes: 6 servings

  ½ **cup butter, cubed**
  ½ **cup packed brown sugar**
  1 **tsp. vanilla extract**
  1 **medium blood orange, thinly sliced**
  1 **sheet frozen puff pastry, thawed**
     Vanilla ice cream, optional

1. Preheat oven to 400°. In an 8-in. cast-iron or other skillet, melt butter over medium heat; stir in the brown sugar and vanilla until dissolved. Arrange orange slices in a single layer over brown sugar.
2. On a lightly floured surface, unfold the puff pastry. Roll to a 9-in. square; place pastry over oranges, tucking in the corners.
3. Bake until golden brown and filling is heated through, 20-25 minutes. Cool 10 minutes before inverting onto a serving plate. Serve warm, with ice cream if desired.
1 piece: 416 cal., 26g fat (12g sat. fat), 41mg chol., 262mg sod., 43g carb. (19g sugars, 3g fiber), 3g pro.

FROZEN LIME CAKE

FROZEN LIME CAKE

We've got just the thing for block parties, cookouts or any time you need a super cool dessert. Making the crust is a snap, and the ice cream and sherbet are so delicious. Everyone loves it!
—Kathy Gillogly, Sun City, CA

- -

Prep: 15 min. + freezing
Makes: 9 servings

  1½ **cups ground almonds**
  ¾ **cup crushed gingersnap cookies (about 15 cookies)**
  ⅓ **cup butter, melted**
  2 **pints pineapple-coconut or vanilla ice cream, softened**
  2 **pints lime sherbet, softened**
     Whipped topping, optional

1. In a small bowl, combine almonds, cookies and butter. Press onto the bottom of a 9-in. square pan. Freeze 15 minutes.
2. Spread ice cream over the crust. Cover and freeze at least 30 minutes. Top with sherbet. Cover and freeze 4 hours or overnight.
3. Remove from freezer 10 minutes before serving. Garnish pieces with whipped topping if desired.
1 piece (calculated without whipped topping): 499 cal., 29g fat (13g sat. fat), 98mg chol., 203mg sod., 54g carb. (40g sugars, 4g fiber), 8g pro.

WATERMELON BOMBE DESSERT

WATERMELON BOMBE DESSERT

When cut, this sherbet dessert looks like an actual watermelon slice—complete with seeds. It is refreshing and fun to eat. Slightly soften each flavor of sherbet before adding it.

—Renae Moncur, Burley, ID

- -

Prep: 20 min. + freezing
Makes: 8 servings

About 1 pint lime sherbet
About 1 pint pineapple sherbet
About 1½ pints raspberry sherbet
¼ cup miniature semisweet chocolate chips

1. Line a 1½-qt. bowl with plastic wrap. Press lime sherbet against bottom and sides of bowl. Freeze, uncovered, until firm.
2. Spread the pineapple sherbet evenly over the lime sherbet layer. Freeze, uncovered, until firm. (The lime and pineapple sherbet layers should be thin.)
3. Pack raspberry sherbet in the center of the sherbet-lined bowl. Smooth the top to resemble a cut watermelon. Cover and freeze until firm, about 8 hours.
4. Just before serving, uncover bowl of molded sherbet. Place a serving plate on the bowl and invert. Remove bowl and peel off the plastic wrap.
5. Cut the bombe into wedges; press a few of the chocolate chips into the raspberry section of each wedge to resemble watermelon seeds.

1 piece: 205 cal., 4g fat (2g sat. fat), 8mg chol., 60mg sod., 43g carb. (35g sugars, 0 fiber), 2g pro.

TOFFEE POKE CAKE

This recipe is a favorite among my family and friends. I love making it because it is so simple.

—Jeanette Hoffman, Oshkosh, WI

- -

Prep: 25 min.
Bake: 25 min. + chilling
Makes: 15 servings

- 1 pkg. chocolate cake mix (regular size)
- 1 jar (17 oz.) butterscotch-caramel ice cream topping
- 1 carton (12 oz.) frozen whipped topping, thawed
- 3 Heath candy bars (1.4 oz. each), chopped

1. Prepare and bake cake according to the package directions, using a greased 13x9-in. baking pan. Cool on a wire rack.

2. Using handle of a wooden spoon, poke holes in cake. Pour ¾ cup of the caramel topping into holes. Spoon the remaining caramel topping over the cake. Top with whipped topping. Sprinkle with candy. Refrigerate for at least 2 hours before serving.

1 piece: 404 cal., 16g fat (8g sat. fat), 48mg chol., 322mg sod., 60g carb. (39g sugars, 1g fiber), 4g pro.

CANDY CORN PUDDING POPS

Bring on the fall fun with these easy-peasy frozen treats. A few drops of food coloring make each pop look just like candy corn, but feel free to switch up the colors to match your event.

—*Taste of Home* Test Kitchen

- -

Prep: 20 min. + freezing
Makes: 8 pops

- 2 cups 2% milk
- ½ cup heavy whipping cream
- 1 pkg. (3.4 oz.) instant cheesecake pudding mix
- 4 drops orange food coloring
- 3 drops yellow food coloring
- 8 freezer pop molds or 8 paper cups (3 oz. each) and wooden pop sticks

1. In a bowl, whisk the milk, cream and pudding mix until blended. Let stand for 5 minutes or until soft-set.

2. Divide pudding into 3 bowls. Add yellow food coloring to 1 bowl and orange to another. Pipe or pour mixture in layers into molds or cups. Top molds with holders. If using cups, top with foil and insert sticks through foil. Freeze until firm.

1 pop: 125 cal., 7g fat (4g sat. fat), 22mg chol., 201mg sod., 12g carb. (12g sugars, 0 fiber), 2g pro.

TOFFEE POKE CAKE

**APPLE-SPICE
ANGEL FOOD CAKE**

APPLE-SPICE ANGEL FOOD CAKE

*Angel food cake mix is lower in
fat and calories than regular cake
mix. Apple pie spice and toasted
nuts add a festive fall flavor.*
—Joan Buehnerkemper, Teutopolis, IL

- -

Prep: 10 min.
Bake: 35 min. + cooling
Makes: 16 servings

 1 **pkg. (16 oz.) angel food cake
    mix**
 1 **cup water**
 ⅔ **cup unsweetened applesauce**
 ½ **cup finely chopped pecans,
    toasted**
 1 **tsp. apple pie spice**
    **Optional: Reduced-fat
    whipped topping and/or
    apple slices**

1. In a large bowl, combine cake mix
and water. Beat on low speed for
30 seconds. Beat on medium speed
for 1 minute. Fold in the applesauce,
pecans and pie spice.
2. Gently spoon into an ungreased
10-in. tube pan. Cut through batter
with a knife to remove air pockets.
Bake on the lowest oven rack at 350°
for 35-45 minutes or until lightly
browned and entire top appears
dry. Immediately invert pan; cool
completely, about 1 hour.
3. Run a knife around the side and
center tube of pan. Remove cake to
a serving plate. Garnish with whipped
topping and/or apple slices if desired.
1 piece: 136 cal., 3g fat (0 sat. fat),
0 chol., 209mg sod., 26g carb. (14g
sugars, 1g fiber), 3g pro.

FLOURLESS CHOCOLATE TORTE

FLOURLESS CHOCOLATE TORTE

Here's the perfect dessert for chocoholics—like me! I bake this melt-in-your-mouth torte all the time for special occasions. For an elegant finish, dust it with confectioners' sugar.
—Kayla Albrecht, Freeport, IL

Prep: 20 min.
Bake: 40 min. + cooling
Makes: 12 servings

- 5 large eggs, separated
- 12 oz. semisweet chocolate, chopped
- ¾ cup butter, cubed
- ¼ tsp. cream of tartar
- ½ cup sugar
  Confectioners' sugar, optional

1. Place egg whites in a large bowl; let stand at room temperature for 30 minutes. Preheat oven to 350°. In the top of a double boiler or in a metal bowl over barely simmering water, melt chocolate and butter; stir until smooth. Remove from heat; cool slightly.

2. In another large bowl, beat egg yolks until thick and lemon-colored. Beat in chocolate mixture. With clean beaters, beat egg whites and cream of tartar on medium speed until foamy.

3. Gradually add sugar, 1 Tbsp. at a time, beating on high after each addition until sugar is dissolved. Continue beating until stiff glossy peaks form. Fold a fourth of the egg whites into chocolate mixture, then fold in the remaining whites

4. Transfer batter to a greased 9-in. springform pan. Bake until a toothpick inserted in center comes out with moist crumbs, 40-45 minutes (do not overbake). Cool completely on a wire rack.

5. Loosen sides from pan with a knife. Remove rim. If desired, dust with confectioners' sugar.

1 piece: 326 cal., 24g fat (14g sat. fat), 108mg chol., 121mg sod., 15g carb. (14g sugars, 1g fiber), 5g pro.

CHOCOLATE LOVER'S PIZZA

CHOCOLATE LOVER'S PIZZA

I created this after my dad said that my graham cracker crust should be topped with dark chocolate and pecans. It's easy to customize by adding your favorite chocolate and toppers. Dad thinks the whole world should know about this pizza!

—Kathy Rairigh, Milford, IN

- -

Prep: 10 min.
Bake: 10 min. + chilling
Makes: 16 pieces

2½   **cups graham cracker crumbs**
⅔   **cup butter, melted**
½   **cup sugar**
2   **pkg. Dove dark chocolate candies (9½ oz. each)**
½   **cup chopped pecans**

1. Preheat oven to 375°. Combine cracker crumbs, butter and sugar; press onto a greased 12-in. pizza pan.
2. Bake 7-9 minutes or until lightly browned. Top with chocolate candies; bake 2-3 minutes longer or until the chocolate is softened.
3. Spread chocolate over crust; sprinkle with nuts. Cool on a wire rack for 15 minutes. Refrigerate for 1-2 hours or until set.
1 piece: 349 cal., 23g fat (12g sat. fat), 24mg chol., 133mg sod., 37g carb. (26g sugars, 3g fiber), 3g pro.

TOASTED COCONUT MILK SHAKES

I created this simple recipe as a reminder of my oldest brother, Brad, who was a picky eater but who loved any dessert that had coconut in it. It has a short list of ingredients, but it's certainly long on coconut flavor!

—Laurie Hudson, Westville, FL

- -

Takes: 15 min. • **Makes:** 4 servings

½   **cup flaked coconut**
⅔   **cup coconut milk, stirred before measuring then chilled**
½   **cup cream of coconut, stirred before measuring then chilled**
4   **cups vanilla ice cream**
    Sweetened whipped cream

1. In a small skillet, cook and stir coconut over medium-low heat until toasted, 6-8 minutes. Let cool completely.
2. Place coconut milk, cream of coconut, ¼ cup toasted coconut and the ice cream in a blender; cover and process until blended.
3. Pour into 4 glasses. Top with whipped cream; sprinkle with the remaining ¼ cup of toasted coconut. Serve immediately.
1 cup: 502 cal., 30g fat (23g sat. fat), 58mg chol., 161mg sod., 54g carb. (51g sugars, 1g fiber), 6g pro.

TOASTED COCONUT
MILK SHAKES

COOL & CREAMY WATERMELON PIE

This simple pie is so refreshing that it never lasts long on warm summer days. Watermelon and a few convenience items make it a delightful dessert that's easy to whip up.

—Velma Beck, Carlinville, IL

- -

Prep: 15 min. + chilling
Makes: 8 servings

- 1   pkg. (3 oz.) watermelon gelatin
- ¼   cup boiling water
- 1   carton (12 oz.) frozen whipped topping, thawed
- 2   cups cubed seeded watermelon
- 1   graham cracker crust (9 in.)

1. In a large bowl, dissolve gelatin in the boiling water. Cool liquid to room temperature.
2. Whisk in whipped topping; fold in watermelon. Spoon into crust. Refrigerate for 2 hours or until set.
1 piece: 272 cal., 12g fat (8g sat. fat), 0 chol., 147mg sod., 36g carb. (27g sugars, 1g fiber), 2g pro.

PEACH CRISP DELIGHT

I love crisps, and this one is a cinch to whip up. The Rice Chex makes it unique, while peaches and brown sugar provide loads of classic appeal. Better still, it takes less than 30 minutes from start to finish!

—Tracy Golder, Bloomsburg, PA

- -

Takes: 25 min. • **Makes:** 6 servings

- 2   cans (15 oz. each) sliced peaches, drained
- 2   cups Rice Chex, crushed
- ⅓   cup packed brown sugar
- ¼   cup all-purpose flour
- 3   Tbsp. cold butter
       Optional: Whipped topping or ice cream

1. Preheat oven to 375°. Place the peaches in a greased 8-in. square baking dish. In a small bowl, combine the cereal, brown sugar and flour; cut in the butter until the mixture resembles coarse crumbs. Sprinkle over peaches.
2. Bake, uncovered, 15-20 minutes or until topping is golden brown. Serve warm.
1 serving: 222 cal., 6g fat (4g sat. fat), 15mg chol., 125mg sod., 41g carb. (30g sugars, 1g fiber), 1g pro.

PEACH CRISP DELIGHT

RED VELVET
CAKE BITES

❄ RED VELVET CAKE BITES

Everyone loves red velvet, but any cake mix can work here. I've rolled chopped macadamia nuts into pineapple cake and dipped them into white chocolate. Whatever you do, have fun!
—Anne Powers, Munford, AL

Prep: 45 min. + chilling
Bake: 25 min. + cooling
Makes: 5 dozen

- 1 pkg. red velvet cake mix (regular size)
- 1 can (16 oz.) cream cheese frosting
- 1 lb. each white, milk chocolate and dark chocolate candy coating

1. Prepare and bake cake mix according to package directions, using a 13x9-in. baking pan. Cool completely.

2. Crumble cake into a large bowl. Add frosting; beat well. Refrigerate until easy to handle, about 1 hour. Shape into 1½-in. balls; transfer to waxed paper-lined baking sheets. Refrigerate at least 1 hour.

3. In a microwave, melt white candy coating; stir until smooth. Dip first 20 cake balls into the coating; allow excess to drip off. Return to baking sheets; let stand until set. Repeat with the milk chocolate and dark chocolate coatings and remaining cake balls. If desired, drizzle with additional candy coating. Store in airtight containers.

Freeze option: Freeze uncoated cake balls in freezer containers, layered between waxed paper. To use, thaw in covered containers. Dip in coatings as directed.

Note: Also known as confectionery coating, candy coating is tempered, ready for melting and sets up quickly at room temperature. It is available in blocks or disks at grocery stores.

1 cake ball: 206 cal., 11g fat (7g sat. fat), 11mg chol., 79mg sod., 28g carb. (24g sugars, 0 fiber), 1g pro.

CINNAMON MONKEY BREAD

Is it possible for four kids to cook together without total chaos in the kitchen? Yes, with the right recipe! This is a favorite with my bunch. They get to play as they roll refrigerated biscuit dough into balls. Then they get to enjoy the results!

—Lisa Combs, Greenville, OH

- -

Prep: 20 min. • **Bake:** 35 min.
Makes: 16 servings

4 tubes (7½ oz. each) refrigerated buttermilk biscuits
½ cup sugar
2 tsp. ground cinnamon
½ cup butter, melted
½ cup packed brown sugar

1. Preheat oven to 350°. Cut each biscuit into 4 pieces; shape into balls. Combine sugar and cinnamon. Roll each ball in cinnamon sugar. Arrange balls evenly in a generously greased 9- or 10-in. fluted tube pan. Sprinkle with remaining cinnamon sugar.

2. Combine butter and brown sugar; pour over the top. Place tube pan on baking sheet; bake until the dough is golden brown and cooked through, 35-45 minutes.

3. Cool in pan for 5 minutes before inverting cake onto a serving platter.

1 piece: 133 cal., 6g fat (4g sat. fat), 15mg chol., 174mg sod., 19g carb. (13g sugars, 0 fiber), 1g pro.

LEMON MERINGUE FLOATS

I dreamed of this float idea one night and woke up knowing I needed to make it. Thank you, Mr. Sandman!

—Cindy Reams, Philipsburg, PA

Takes: 5 min. • **Makes:** 6 servings

- 3 cups vanilla ice cream, softened if necessary
- 18 miniature meringue cookies
- 6 cups cold pink lemonade

Place ½ cup ice cream and 3 cookies in each of 6 tall glasses. Top with lemonade. Serve immediately.

1½ cups with 3 cookies: 282 cal., 7g fat (4g sat. fat), 29mg chol., 77mg sod., 51g carb. (48g sugars, 0 fiber), 3g pro.

TEST KITCHEN TIP
Make your floats with frozen yogurt for a slimmed-down treat.

LEMON MERINGUE FLOATS

HAZELNUT MOCHA
SMOOTHIES

HAZELNUT MOCHA SMOOTHIES

This smooth blend of coffee, cocoa and nutty flavors is better than any coffeehouse version we've tried. Try it, and we're sure you will agree.

—*Taste of Home* Test Kitchen

- -

Takes: 10 min. • **Makes:** 3 servings

- 1 **cup 2% milk**
- ½ **cup Nutella**
- 4 **tsp. instant espresso powder**
- 6 **ice cubes**
- 2 **cups vanilla ice cream**
  Chocolate curls, optional

In a blender, combine milk, Nutella and espresso powder; cover and process until blended. Add the ice cubes; cover and process until smooth. Add ice cream; cover and process until smooth. Pour into chilled glasses; serve immediately. Garnish with chocolate curls if desired.

1 cup: 474 cal., 27g fat (10g sat. fat), 47mg chol., 124mg sod., 55g carb. (46g sugars, 2g fiber), 9g pro.

RASPBERRY SWIRLED CHEESECAKE PIE

My dad always said that my cheesecake pie was his favorite dessert. He is gone now but I remember his smile every time I make it.

—Peggy Griffin, Elba, NE

- -

Prep: 15 min.
Bake: 35 min. + chilling
Makes: 8 servings

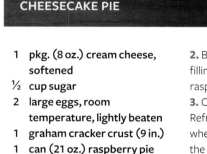

RASPBERRY SWIRLED CHEESECAKE PIE

- 1 **pkg. (8 oz.) cream cheese, softened**
- ½ **cup sugar**
- 2 **large eggs, room temperature, lightly beaten**
- 1 **graham cracker crust (9 in.)**
- 1 **can (21 oz.) raspberry pie filling, divided**

1. Preheat oven to 350°. In a large bowl, beat cream cheese and sugar until smooth. Add eggs; beat on low speed just until blended. Pour into the crust. Drop ½ cup pie filling by tablespoonfuls over batter. Cut through batter with a knife to swirl.

2. Bake 35-45 minutes or until the filling is set. Refrigerate remaining raspberry filling in covered container.

3. Cool pie 1 hour on a wire rack. Refrigerate at least 2 hours, covering when completely cooled. Serve with the reserved filling.

1 piece: 337 cal., 16g fat (8g sat. fat), 84mg chol., 253mg sod., 44g carb. (33g sugars, 2g fiber), 5g pro.

PRESSURE-COOKER
CHOCOLATE-APRICOT
DUMP CAKE

PRESSURE-COOKER CHOCOLATE-APRICOT DUMP CAKE

Years ago, I used to prepare a dessert similar to this in the oven. I converted it to my Instant Pot and now we can enjoy it quickly. Try it with white cake mix and blueberry pie filling, too. It's best served warm with ice cream or whipped cream.

—Joan Hallford,
North Richland Hills, TX

- -

Prep: 10 min.
Cook: 35 min. + standing
Makes: 8 servings

1   can (21 oz.) apricot or peach pie filling
2   cups devil's food cake mix
½   cup chopped pecans, toasted
½   cup miniature semisweet chocolate chips, optional
½   cup butter, cubed
Vanilla ice cream, optional

1. Place trivet insert and 1 cup water in a 6-qt. electric pressure cooker. Spread pie filling in the bottom of a greased 1½-qt. baking dish. Sprinkle with cake mix, pecans and, if desired, chocolate chips. Dot with butter. Cover baking dish with foil.

2. Fold an 18x12-in. piece of foil lengthwise into thirds, making a sling. Use the sling to lower the dish onto the trivet. Lock lid; close pressure-release valve. Adjust to pressure-cook on high for 35 minutes. Quick-release pressure. Press cancel.

3. Using the foil sling, carefully remove the baking dish. Let stand 10 minutes. If desired, serve warm cake with ice cream.

1 serving: 360 cal., 18g fat (9g sat. fat), 31mg chol., 436mg sod., 49g carb. (26g sugars, 1g fiber), 2g pro.

STRAWBERRY POKE CAKE

Strawberry shortcake takes on a wonderful new twist with this super simple recipe. Strawberries liven up each pretty slice.

—Mary Jo Griggs, West Bend, WI

Prep: 25 min.
Bake: 25 min. + chilling
Makes: 12 servings

- 1 pkg. white cake mix (regular size)
- 1¼ cups water
- 2 large eggs, room temperature
- ¼ cup canola oil
- 2 pkg. (10 oz. each) frozen sweetened sliced strawberries, thawed
- 2 pkg. (3 oz. each) strawberry gelatin
- 1 carton (12 oz.) frozen whipped topping, thawed, divided
  Fresh strawberries, optional

1. Preheat oven to 350°. In a large bowl, combine the cake mix, water, eggs and oil; beat on low speed for 30 seconds. Beat on medium for 2 minutes.

2. Pour into 2 greased and floured 9-in. round baking pans. Bake until a toothpick inserted in the center comes out clean, 25-35 minutes. Cool 10 minutes; remove from pans to wire racks to cool completely.

3. Using a serrated knife, level tops of cakes if necessary. Return layers, top side up, to 2 clean 9-in. round baking pans. Pierce cakes with a meat fork or wooden skewer at ½-in. intervals.

4. Drain the juice from strawberries into a 2-cup container; refrigerate berries. Add water to the juice to measure 2 cups; pour into a small saucepan. Bring to a boil; stir in the gelatin until dissolved. Chill liquid for 30 minutes. Gently spoon over each cake layer. Chill for 2-3 hours.

5. Dip bottom of 1 pan into warm water for 10 seconds, then invert onto a serving platter. Top with chilled strawberries and 1 cup of whipped topping. Place second cake layer over topping.

6. Frost cake with the remaining whipped topping. Chill cake at least 1 hour. Serve with fresh berries if desired. Refrigerate leftovers.

1 piece: 376 cal., 14g fat (7g sat. fat), 35mg chol., 301mg sod., 56g carb. (37g sugars, 1g fiber), 4g pro

STRAWBERRY POKE CAKE

★ ★ ★ ★ ★ **READER REVIEW**

"Light and refreshing cake to serve. I'd rate this cake one of the best...and I've cooked and baked for years!"

—CARLAGREENE, TASTEOFHOME.COM

CHERRY CREAM CHEESE TARTS

CHERRY CREAM CHEESE TARTS

It's hard to believe that just five ingredients and a few minutes of preparation can result in these delicate and scrumptious tarts!
—Cindi Mitchell, Waring, TX

Takes: 10 min. • **Makes:** 2 tarts

> 3 oz. cream cheese, softened
> ¼ cup confectioners' sugar
> ⅛ to ¼ tsp. almond or vanilla extract
> 2 individual graham cracker shells
> ¼ cup cherry pie filling

In a small bowl, beat the cream cheese, sugar and vanilla extract until smooth. Spoon into shells. Top with pie filling. Refrigerate until serving.

1 tart: 362 cal., 20g fat (10g sat. fat), 43mg chol., 265mg sod., 42g carb. (29g sugars, 1g fiber), 4g pro.

★ ★ ★ ★ ★ **READER REVIEW**

"A fast and easy dessert that tastes delicious. I like to have the ingredients on hand for a quick weeknight treat."
—LVARNER, TASTEOFHOME.COM

**ALL-AMERICAN
SHEET CAKE**

ALL-AMERICAN
SHEET CAKE

*My sweet and tangy sheet
cake piled with fresh whipped
cream and juicy fruit is so good,
you might just want to eat it
for breakfast.*

—James Schend, Pleasant Prairie, WI

- -

Prep: 20 min.
Bake: 25 min. + cooling
Makes: 15 servings

1 **pkg. white cake mix
  (regular size)**
1 **cup buttermilk**
⅓ **cup canola oil**
3 **large eggs, room
  temperature**
2 **to 3 cups sweetened
  whipped cream**
3 **to 4 cups assorted
  fresh fruit**

1. Preheat oven to 350°. Combine
cake mix, buttermilk, oil and eggs;
beat on low speed for 30 seconds.
Beat on medium for 2 minutes.

2. Pour into a 13x9-in. baking pan
coated with cooking spray. Bake until
a toothpick inserted in the center
comes out clean, 25-30 minutes.
Cool completely on a wire rack.
3. Spread whipped cream over
cake; top with fruit. Refrigerate.
Note: To substitute for buttermilk,
use 1 Tbsp. white vinegar or lemon
juice plus enough milk to measure
1 cup. Stir, then let stand 5 minutes.
Or, use 1 cup plain yogurt or 1¾ tsp.
cream of tartar plus 1 cup milk.
1 piece: 257 cal., 15g fat (5g sat. fat),
56mg chol., 261mg sod., 29g carb.
(14g sugars, 0 fiber), 4g pro.

CHOCOLATE MOLTEN CAKES

cakes for 17-20 minutes or until a thermometer inserted in the center reads 160°and sides of cakes are set.

4. Remove from oven; let stand for 1 minute. Run a knife around sides of ramekins; invert onto dessert plates. Serve immediately.

1 cake: 877 cal., 68g fat (39g sat. fat), 359mg chol., 255mg sod., 67g carb. (60g sugars, 7g fiber), 12g pro.

RED, WHITE & BLUE TORTE

My guests see fireworks when I turn a frozen pound cake into this patriotic pleaser! Assemble the tempting torte early in the day and keep it in the refrigerator until it's time for dessert.

—Margery Bryan, Moses Lake, WA

- -

Prep: 10 min. + chilling
Makes: 8 pieces

- 1 loaf (10¾ oz.) frozen pound cake, thawed
- ½ cup blueberry pie filling
- ½ cup strawberry or raspberry pie filling
- 1¾ cups whipped topping

1. Cut cake horizontally into 3 layers. Place the bottom layer on a serving platter; spread with blueberry filling. Top with middle cake layer; spread with strawberry filling. replace top of cake.

2. Frost top and sides with whipped topping. Refrigerate for several hours before slicing.

1 piece: 222 cal., 9g fat (6g sat. fat), 54mg chol., 148mg sod., 32g carb. (19g sugars, 1g fiber), 3g pro.

CHOCOLATE MOLTEN CAKES

Be prepared to swoon when you dip into this indulgent flourless cake and warm chocolate oozes from its center. It was one of the favorite desserts on the menu at La Boucherie restaurant. Try it, and you'll understand why!

—Matthew Lawrence, Vashon, WA

- -

Takes: 30 min. • **Makes:** 6 servings

- 2 tsp. plus 1 cup butter, cubed, divided
- 6 tsp. plus ¼ cup sugar, divided
- 1¼ lbs. semisweet chocolate, chopped
- 2 large eggs, room temperature
- 6 large egg yolks, room temperature

1. Preheat oven to 350°. Grease six 6-oz. ramekins or custard cups with 2 tsp. butter. Sprinkle the sides and bottoms of each ramekin with 1 tsp. sugar; set aside.

2. In the top of a double boiler or a metal bowl over hot water, melt chocolate and remaining butter; stir until smooth. Remove from heat. In a large bowl, beat eggs, egg yolks and the remaining ¼ cup sugar until thick and lemon-colored. With a spatula, fold half of the egg mixture into chocolate mixture just until blended. Fold in the remaining egg mixture.

3. Transfer to prepared ramekins. Place on a baking sheet. Bake

RED, WHITE
& BLUE TORTE

PEACH CREAM PIE

My family loves this dessert and asks for it often. It's a breeze to make and delicious served warm or cold.

—Karen Odom, Melbourne, FL

- -

Prep: 10 min. • **Bake:** 40 min.
Makes: 8 pieces

- 6 medium ripe peaches, peeled and sliced
- 1 sheet refrigerated pie pastry
- ½ cup sugar
- 3 Tbsp. all-purpose flour
- ¼ tsp. salt
- ¾ cup heavy whipping cream

1. Preheat oven to 400°. Unroll dough; transfer to a 9-in. deep-dish pie plate.
2. Arrange peaches in crust. In a small bowl, combine sugar, flour and salt; stir in cream until smooth. Pour over peaches.
3. Bake until filling is almost set, 40-45 minutes. Serve warm or cold. Refrigerate leftovers.

1 piece: 413 cal., 25g fat (16g sat. fat), 68 mg chol., 287mg sod., 45g carb. (22g sugars, 2g fiber), 5g pro.

SLOW-COOKER STRAWBERRY PUDDING CAKE

I had these ingredients in my pantry and thought I'd experiment—the flavors are just like strawberry cheesecake, only in a warm, comforting cake version. It's a whole lot easier than making cheesecake, too!

—Lisa Renshaw, Kansas City, MO

- -

Prep: 20 min.
Cook: 4 hours + standing
Makes: 10 servings

- 3 cups cold 2% milk
- 1 pkg. (3.4 oz.) instant cheesecake or vanilla pudding mix
- 1 pkg. strawberry cake mix (regular size)
- 1 cup water
- 3 large eggs, room temperature
- ⅓ cup canola oil
- 2 cups toasted coconut marshmallows, quartered
- Optional: Strawberry ice cream topping and sliced fresh strawberries

1. In a large bowl, whisk milk and pudding mix for 2 minutes. Transfer to a greased 4- or 5-qt. slow cooker. Prepare cake mix batter according to package directions with water, eggs and oil; pour over the pudding layer.
2. Cook, covered, on low until the edges of the cake are golden brown (center will be moist), about 4 hours.
3. Remove the slow-cooker insert; sprinkle cake with marshmallows. Let stand, uncovered, for 10 minutes before serving. If desired, serve with ice cream topping and strawberries.

1 serving: 377 cal., 13g fat (4g sat. fat), 62mg chol., 540mg sod., 56g carb. (37g sugars, 1g fiber), 6g pro.

SLOW-COOKER STRAWBERRY PUDDING CAKE

SOPAIPILLAS

SOPAIPILLAS

Light and crispy pastry puffs, sopaipillas are a sweet way to round out a spicy meal. We love to serve them warm and top them off with honey or sugar.

—Mary Anne McWhirter, Pearland, TX

- -

Prep: 15 min. + standing
Cook: 25 min. • **Makes:** 1 dozen

- 1   cup all-purpose flour
- 1½ tsp. baking powder
- ¼   tsp. salt
- 1   Tbsp. shortening
- ⅓   cup warm water
  Oil for deep-fat frying
  Optional: Confectioners'
  sugar and honey

1. In a large bowl, combine flour, baking powder and salt. Cut in shortening until mixture resembles fine crumbs. Gradually add water, tossing with a fork until a loose ball forms (dough will be crumbly).

2. On a lightly floured surface, knead the dough for 3 minutes or until smooth. Cover and let rest for 10 minutes.

3. Roll out the rested dough into a 12x10-in. rectangle. Cut into 12 square shapes or use a round biscuit cutter to cut 12 circles .

4. In a deep-fat fryer, heat 2 in. oil to 375°. Fry sopaipillas for 1-2 minutes on each side. Drain on paper towels; keep warm. If desired, dust with confectioners' sugar and/or serve with honey.

1 sopaipilla: 57 cal., 2g fat (0 sat. fat), 0 chol., 109mg sod., 8g carb. (0 sugars, 0 fiber), 1g pro.

DUTCH OVEN CHERRY CHOCOLATE DUMP CAKE

DUTCH OVEN CHERRY CHOCOLATE DUMP CAKE

Looking for a super quick dessert that will make people think you spent all day in the kitchen? This easy dessert will wow your guests. Feel free to use your favorite pie filling in place of cherry.

—Rashanda Cobbins, Milwaukee, WI

- -

Prep: 5 min. • **Bake:** 35 min.
Makes: 8 servings

1 can (21 oz.) cherry pie filling
1 can (12 oz.) evaporated milk
1 pkg. chocolate cake mix (regular size)
⅓ cup sliced almonds
¾ cup butter, melted
Vanilla ice cream, optional

1. Preheat oven to 350°. Line a 4-qt. Dutch oven with parchment; lightly spray with cooking spray. Combine pie filling and evaporated milk; spread the filling mixture on bottom of Dutch oven. Sprinkle with cake mix (unprepared) and almonds; drizzle with butter.

2. Bake, covered, until cake springs back when touched, 35-40 minutes. If desired, serve with ice cream.

1 cup: 515 cal., 24g fat (15g sat. fat), 61mg chol., 605mg sod., 68g carb. (44g sugars, 3g fiber), 7g pro.

ARCTIC ORANGE PIE

*This frosty pie is so easy to make.
I have tried lemonade, mango
and pineapple juice concentrates
instead of orange, and my family
loves each one.*

—Marie Przepierski, Erie, PA

- -

Prep: 20 min. + freezing
Makes: 8 servings

- 1   pkg. (8 oz.) fat-free
  cream cheese
- 1   can (6 oz.) frozen orange
  juice concentrate, thawed
- 1   carton (8 oz.) frozen
  reduced-fat whipped
  topping, thawed
- 1   reduced-fat graham cracker
  crust (9 in.)
- 1   can (11 oz.) mandarin
  oranges, drained

In a large bowl, beat cream cheese
and orange juice concentrate until
smooth. Fold in whipped topping;
pour into crust. Cover and freeze for
4 hours or until firm. Remove from
the freezer about 10 minutes before
cutting. Garnish with oranges.

1 piece: 248 cal., 7g fat (4g sat. fat),
3mg chol., 298mg sod., 35g carb.
(24g sugars, 0 fiber), 6g pro.

ARCTIC ORANGE PIE

EASY KEY LIME PIE

EASY KEY LIME PIE

This refreshing pie is a winner on all counts—it's quick and easy enough to make for a weeknight dessert, but special enough to take to weekend potlucks.
—*Taste of Home* Test Kitchen

Prep: 20 min. + chilling
Makes: 8 servings

- 1 pkg. (8 oz.) cream cheese, softened
- 1 can (14 oz.) sweetened condensed milk
- ½ cup Key lime juice or lime juice
- 1 graham cracker crust (9 in.)
- 2 cups whipped topping
  Lime slices, optional

In a large bowl, beat cream cheese until smooth. Beat in milk and lime juice until blended. Transfer to crust. Refrigerate, covered, at least 4 hours. Just before serving, garnish with whipped topping and, if desired, lime slices.

1 piece: 417 cal., 22g fat (13g sat. fat), 46mg chol., 274mg sod., 48g carb. (42g sugars, 0 fiber), 7g pro.

★ ★ ★ ★ ★ **READER REVIEW**
"This is a fabulous recipe. It's a lot better than store bought! Use Key lime, not lime—the flavor is more authentic."
—MARENESMITH, TASTEOFHOME.COM

DOUGHNUT HOLE CAKE

DOUGHNUT HOLE CAKE

This is the easiest, most impressive cake I've ever made! You can use chocolate, lemon or strawberry cake mix in the place of red velvet if you prefer.
—Robert Pickart, Chicago, IL

Prep: 15 min.
Bake: 35 min. + cooling
Makes: 16 servings

- 32 vanilla cake doughnut holes
- 1 pkg. red velvet cake mix (regular size)
- 1 can (16 oz.) vanilla frosting

1. Preheat oven to 350°. Place 16 doughnut holes in each of 2 greased 8-in. round baking pans. Prepare the cake mix according to package directions. Pour batter over doughnuts, dividing evenly.
2. Bake until a toothpick inserted in the cake comes out clean, 35-40 minutes. Cool in pans for 10 minutes before removing to a wire rack to cool completely. Spread frosting between layers and over top of cake.

1 piece: 420 cal., 20g fat (7g sat. fat), 38mg chol., 401mg sod., 57g carb. (36g sugars, 1g fiber), 4g pro.

PUMPKIN
GINGERSNAP
ICE CREAM PIE

PUMPKIN GINGERSNAP ICE CREAM PIE

My family and I always try new desserts during the holidays. This one was a clear winner at our Christmas party, so we now make it for all occasions!
—Patricia Ness, La Mesa, CA

- -

Prep: 25 min. + freezing
Makes: 8 servings

1½ cups crushed gingersnap
    cookies (about 30 cookies)
2 Tbsp. ground walnuts
1 Tbsp. canola oil
FILLING
4 cups reduced-fat vanilla ice
    cream, softened if necessary
1 cup canned pumpkin pie
    filling
    Pumpkin pie spice

1. Preheat oven to 350°. In a small bowl, mix crushed cookies and ground walnuts; stir in oil. Press mixture onto bottom and up sides of an ungreased 9-in. pie plate. Bake for 8-10 minutes or until set. Cool completely on a wire rack.

2. In a large bowl, mix ice cream and pie filling until blended. Spread into the prepared crust; sprinkle with pie spice. Freeze, covered, 8 hours or overnight.

1 piece: 304 cal., 9g fat (3g sat. fat), 21mg chol., 233mg sod., 50g carb. (29g sugars, 2g fiber), 6g pro.

MILKY WAY PUDGY PIE

My favorite pudgy pies are made with Milky Way candy bars, graham cracker crumbs and marshmallows. Irresistible! And buttered bread is a must.

—Susan Hein, Burlington, WI

- -

Takes: 10 min. • **Makes:** 1 serving

1	Tbsp. butter, softened
2	slices white bread
1	Tbsp. graham cracker crumbs
1	fun-size Milky Way candy bar, chopped
2	Tbsp. miniature marshmallows

1. Spread butter over bread slices. Place 1 slice in a sandwich iron, buttered side down. Top with cracker crumbs, chopped candy, marshmallows and the remaining bread slice, buttered side up. Close iron.

2. Cook over a hot campfire until golden brown and marshmallows are melted, 3-6 minutes, turning occasionally.

1 sandwich: 380 cal., 17g fat (10g sat. fat), 32mg chol., 438mg sod., 51g carb. (19g sugars, 2g fiber), 6g pro.

HOMEMADE CHOCOLATE PUDDING

My mother used to make this dessert whenever she could. During the Depression it was hard to find chocolate, but if she found some, she saved enough to make this pudding. I make it now and think of her every time I prepare it.

—Maribeth Janus, Ivoryton, CT

- -

Takes: 15 min. • **Makes:** 2 servings

2	Tbsp. sugar
1	Tbsp. cornstarch
1	cup 2% milk
⅓	cup semisweet chocolate chips
½	tsp. vanilla extract

1. In a small saucepan, combine sugar and cornstarch. Add the milk; stir until smooth. Cook and stir over medium heat until mixture comes to a boil. Cook and stir until thickened, 1-2 minutes longer.

2. Stir in chocolate chips; cook and stir until melted. Remove from heat. Stir in vanilla. Spoon into dessert dishes. Serve warm or chilled.

½ cup: 275 cal., 12g fat (8g sat. fat), 17mg chol., 63mg sod., 40g carb. (34g sugars, 2g fiber), 5g pro.

MILKY WAY PUDGY PIE

INDEX